THE EDITORS

Oscar James Campbell established the text for this edition and served as the authority on all points of scholarship. Recognized as one of the leading Shakespearean scholars, he is editor of *The Living Shakespeare* and author of *Shakespeare's Satire, Comical Satyre, Shakespeare's Troilus and Cressida,* and numerous other books and articles on literary subjects. Dr. Campbell is now Professor Emeritus of Columbia University; he was formerly Chairman of the English Department.

Alfred Rothschild, writer and lecturer, has an original and penetrating approach to many subjects. A life-long Shakespeare addict, he originated the unique features of the Bantam Shakespeare. He worked on every phase of the project in close contact with the other editors, and supervised the production of the final manuscript.

Stuart Vaughan is one of the country's most prominent theatrical directors. Formerly Artistic Director of the Phoenix Theatre in New York, he is now at the head of the newly established Seattle Repertory Theatre. He staged the Phoenix's highly successful productions of *Hamlet* and *Henry IV, Parts I* and *II.* He was the first director of the New York Shakespeare Festival productions in Central Park, for which he staged *Romeo and Juliet, Macbeth, Two Gentlemen of Verona, Julius Caesar,* and *Othello.* At the Heckscher Theatre in New York, he also directed *Richard III* and *As You Like It.* Mr. Vaughan supervised in particular the stage directions in this edition, wrote the essay on the Elizabethan theatre, and contributed a number of notes.

A MIDSUMMER NIGHT'S DREAM

by

WILLIAM SHAKESPEARE

EDITED BY

OSCAR JAMES CAMPBELL
ALFRED ROTHSCHILD
STUART VAUGHAN

Large Type Edition

 A KEITH JENNISON BOOK

FRANKLIN WATTS, INC., PUBLISHERS
A Division of GROLIER INCORPORATED
575 Lexington Ave. New York, New York 10022

ACKNOWLEDGMENTS

BARBER, C. L.: from *Shakespeare's Festive Comedy*. Reprinted by permission of Princeton University Press. Copyright, 1959, by Princeton University Press.

BRADBROOK, MURIEL C.: from *Shakespeare and Elizabethan Poetry*. Reprinted by permission of Oxford University Press, Inc., and Chatto & Windus, Ltd.

PARROTT, THOMAS M.: from *Shakespearean Comedy*. Russell & Russell, Inc. New York, 1962. Copyright, 1949, by Thomas Marc Parrott.

WELSFORD, ENID: from *The Court Masque*. Reprinted by permission of Cambridge University Press.

Library of Congress Catalog Card Number: 65-17711

The text of this large type edition
is complete and unabridged.

Foreword

BY ALFRED ROTHSCHILD

Still another Shakespeare! To be sure—but a Shakespeare "with a difference."

It all started years ago with a complaint from a high school student. He had seen a performance of *Julius Caesar*, and was intensely excited about it. Then he tried reading the play, and found he just couldn't make any progress. He was disappointed and puzzled. "What makes it so tough?" he asked.

He didn't know he was planting a seed. It was there and then that this edition began to take shape.

The Bantam Shakespeare seeks to provide in a convenient and easily comprehended form as much guidance and information for the student and general reader as is reasonably possible.

This is how we have tried to achieve our objective:

Text

By "text" we mean the words the characters actually speak. While it is true that this text, written in Elizabethan English, contains words and phrases no longer in common usage, allusions to matters and events no longer easily recognized, and various other obscurities, there was never any doubt about

v

one rule: the basic text must not be violated.

So this is not a new text. There are no "improvements," no rewritten lines, no "corrections" of Elizabethan grammar—even though a change might make some lines more easily understood by modern readers. The editors of this edition are all purists—on fundamentals. But it cannot be repeated too often that there is no such thing as a "pure" Shakespeare text—no such thing even as agreement on whether some passages in the plays were written by Shakespeare himself.

There is, however, an authoritative consensus on the basis of which the so-called "Cambridge Edition" was published about one hundred years ago. William Aldis Wright and William George Clark, the editors, were not, of course, trying to improve Shakespeare. What they did, with infinite care and learning, was to reconcile differences in the original quarto and folio texts, to correct printers' errors, and so on, with due regard to the research and opinions of scholars before them. This Cambridge Edition is now almost universally accepted as the standard reading text.

A special edition of the Cambridge Shakespeare, published under the auspices of the same Cambridge editors, is known as the "Globe" edition, and it is this text that for the purposes of the Bantam Shakespeare is regarded as basically sacrosanct. We have made some changes in punctuation, and also in spelling, particularly in substituting the letter "e" for the apostrophe in words like "aimed," in which the "e" is now always silent. Where we do deviate from the text, which is rarely, we explain why in a Note.

Glossary

Unfamiliar and obscure words in the text of the plays are customarily explained in a glossary at the back of the book, or at the foot of the text page. As a rule, there is no indication that a particular word is "glossed." This means that sometimes the reader will stop to hunt in vain, and sometimes fail to look for an explanation when he should—that is, when the modern meaning of a word differs from its Elizabethan meaning. Take the word "weed," for example. It is certainly neither uncommon nor obscure. But as used by Shakespeare in *A Midsummer Night's Dream* it means "garment"; and unless the reader is made aware of this he cannot properly understand the passage in which the word occurs.

Our method is to place an asterisk next to the word that requires clarification, and then to give the equivalent on the same line in the right-hand margin, so that the eye, particularly as it becomes accustomed to the arrangement, can take it in at a glance.

Obviously, these marginal glosses must be kept within certain limits of length, not only for typographical reasons, but also because excessive length would defeat our objective of having the reader absorb the explanation with the least possible interruption of his train of thought.

In some instances, the word in the glossary margin is not simply the modern equivalent of the word marked with an asterisk, as, for instance, on line 13 of the first scene of *Hamlet*. There "rivals" is easily and with reasonable accuracy translated into modern English as "partners." But now take the word "instrument" in the line "Give me the gown.

Where is thy instrument?" (*Julius Caesar*, IV, 3, 239.) "Instrument" is certainly not an unfamiliar word, nor is it used here in an unfamiliar sense. But there is nothing in the preceding lines to indicate that Brutus is referring to a musical instrument. On the stage, this presents no problem, and stage directors through the centuries have known how to convey the information to the audience. But it is different with the reader. He needs help if he is not to be confused and thus lose something of the atmosphere of one of the most charming and effective touches in the play. So we marked "instrument" with an asterisk and printed "*i.e.*, lute" in the margin, fully aware that "lute" is not a definition of "instrument."

It will be noticed that sometimes there is a slight break in the line in which an asterisk occurs. This signifies that the gloss covers more than one word and applies jointly to the two or more words from the break to the asterisk.

Occasionally, two asterisks will be found on one line. When this occurs, the two glosses are separated by a diagonal stroke.

It is interesting to note, incidentally, that very few glosses are needed for an understanding and appreciation of most of the great key passages. This is not an accident: it is part of the genius of Shakespeare. At his greatest, he is at his simplest —or perhaps we should say that he then achieves that simplicity of effect which hides the infinite complexity of perfection.

Stage Directions

Here we have a situation entirely different from that which applies to the text. Stage directions are simply not text at all.

They are not part of the poetry, the characterization, the dramatic vigor of the lines, which are the glory of Shakespeare. The stage directions that have come down to us from the quartos and folios are almost certainly only the brief markings in the prompt books used in the early staging of the plays. It was not until nearly one hundred years after Shakespeare's death that an edition, edited by Nicholas Rowe, was published, incorporating systematic division into acts and scenes, and many new stage directions.

The history of presenting Shakespeare in print is long. Progress has been difficult and slow. It took many years to change even such externals as Elizabethan spelling and typography. The time has come to take a further step forward by bringing other externals such as stage directions up to date.

The obvious function of stage directions in a reading edition is to help the reader follow the action of the play. There should be an adequate description of the scenes and of the way the characters move about. Our rule has been to follow the Globe edition directions, but to amplify them where necessary, and to modernize the language, and also to paragraph speeches in accordance with their context. In the few instances where we have deemed it essential to go beyond this in order to help the reader understand what is going on, we have called attention to the change in a Note.

In all cases the stage directions are as simple and direct as we could make them. Mood-setting imagery has no place here, any more than a description of a character's state of mind. That would be tantamount to interpreting the character for the reader. Actually, every effort has been made to avoid interpretation. The purpose is not to get in the reader's way, but to illuminate it. The text must be allowed to speak for itself, so that the reader can make his own interpretation as he progresses with his reading. Not that the Bantam Shakespeare neglects interpretation—on the contrary, it makes a special feature of interpretative comment. But it does so where it belongs: in the appendix.

What must be made clear is the difference between a reading version of a Shakespeare play, where stage directions that interpret character are wrong, and a stage or acting version where they are not only right but also essential—and, indeed, inevitable.

Even though the standard division into scenes and acts admittedly leaves something to be desired, we have adhered to it. Nothing substantial is to be gained by changing or eliminating it, but much to be lost, since it is used in the important reference works, such as Schmidt's Lexicon and Bartlett's Concordance.

For an example of our use of stage directions we refer you to Act III, Scene 2, lines 401 to 430. On the stage this is a highly entertaining scene, but the way it is usually presented to the reader makes it unnecessarily difficult for him to appreciate what is going on. The stage directions we have added remedy this: they make it clear how step by step the mischievous Puck befogs and bewilders Demetrius and Lysander until they fall asleep exhausted.

Note, too, how the glosses function. In the first forty lines of Act II, "pale," "pensioners," "lob," "passing," "fell," "trace," "square," "shrewd," "quern," "bootless," "barm," are all terms which must be understood in the sense in which Shakespeare used them if this important scene is to be fully understood. With the Bantam method of glossing, you do not interrupt your reading eleven times: the clarifying meaning, fitting into the grammatical construction of the line, is right there under your eye for your instant use. Thus the thread of your thinking is not broken: your mind, to quote from a particularly pregnant comment by Samuel Johnson, is not "refrigerated" by interruptions.

Notes

Here, too, the aim of the Bantam Shakespeare is maximum reader convenience. The words or passages requiring Notes are consecutively numbered. The Notes in the appendix are numbered in rotation, and also identified by the number of the line. In addition, the number of the page on which the Note is to be found is given in the heading at the top of the page on which the passage occurs. Thus, the reader knows at once not only that there is a Note, but where to find it conveniently and quickly. All the Notes have been written to meet our special objectives. We have tried to keep them succinct, without limiting them in either length or number.

Commentaries

The inclusion of a wide range of commentaries with each play is another important feature of these Bantam editions. But we go still further. We have tied the commentaries together by means of introductory paragraphs. This is important because comment written in the eighteenth century, for example, should not be viewed in the same light as comment written, say, one hundred years later. Some of Voltaire's criticism sounds preposterous today, but the fact is that it cannot be properly evaluated without consideration of the historical and literary background against which it was written.

Format

A great deal of thought has been given to typographical arrangement. The practice of abbreviating character names, so that "Hélena" becomes "Hel," and "Hippolyta," "Hip," is not only esthetically disturbing but often seriously confusing —as when you have "Macd" for "Macduff" on one line, and "Macb" for "Macbeth" on the next. In the Bantam Shakespeare, the name of the character speaking is printed in full and on a separate line. This not only helps to open up the printing in general, but also has the highly desirable effect of reducing the number of run-over lines. All other details, such as the placing of parenthetical stage directions, and the numbering of the lines, have been handled so as to achieve maximum reading ease.

Other Features

Preceding each play is an essay by Professor Campbell written especially for this edition. It analyzes the play, and gives details regarding the source of the plot, the date of composition, and so on. We have also added an annotated bibliography and a chronological table, both prepared by Professor Campbell. The chronological table, bringing as it does events in Shakespeare's life into relation with other events of the time, makes enlightening and fascinating reading. Even a casual glance reveals that Galileo was born in the same year as Shakespeare; that Shakespeare was thirteen at the time of the publication of Holinshed's *Chronicles of England, Scotland, and Ireland*, on which he drew so heavily for his historical plays; and twenty-four at the time of the defeat of the Spanish Armada.

It is important for the reader to know something about the difference between our modern stage and that for which Shakespeare wrote. An essay on the Elizabethan theatre, written by Mr. Stuart Vaughan, has therefore been included.

While the functions of the three editors are clearly defined on the title page, it should be said that the final manuscript emerged as the result of much reviewing of scripts and many conferences involving all the editors. Among these, we must in all fairness include Donald Reis of Bantam Books, whose help in every respect proved invaluable. In actual practice there was no sharp separation of function. So much is here as a result of a harmonious exchange of views of a blending of ideas in the action and reaction of open-minded discussion, that it is impossible to tell where one contribution begins and the other leaves off.

About two hundred years ago, Samuel Johnson wrote:

> Let him that is yet unacquainted with the powers of Shakespeare, and who desires to feel the greatest pleasure that the drama can give, read every play from the first scene to the last, with utter negligence of all his commentators. When his fancy is once on the wing, let it not stop at correction or explanation. When his attention is strongly engaged, let it disdain alike to turn aside to the name of Theobald and of Pope. Let him read on through the brightness and obscurity, through integrity and corruption; let him preserve his comprehension of the dialogue and his interest in the fable. And when the pleasures of novelty have ceased, let him attempt exactness and read the commentators. . . .

The advice is good. Countless commentators have written countless words on the precise meaning of countless terms and phrases, with countless varieties of interpretation. It has not been possible, if only because of space limitations, to do more than indicate some of the more prominent controversial issues.

If you want to venture further, you will do well to use our bibliography as a guide. But always remember that the Why and Wherefore of Shakespeare is part of the mystery of the universe. Learn to enjoy him as a poet and a dramatist. Regard him as you would a magnificent view of land and sea, comprehending an infinite variety of light and shade and color, to which you open up your heart and soul and mind, and let it work its wonders upon you.

Contents

Introduction

BY OSCAR JAMES CAMPBELL

The existing text of the play is the version written in 1594–1595 to be presented in the great hall of an Elizabethan gentleman's country house or perhaps at the Court itself, on an occasion at which the Queen was present. But this portion of the fantasy is only part of one of two textual layers. The older level is represented principally by the dialogue of the lovers and other passages of wooden rhymed verse that Shakespeare must have written at the very beginning of his dramatic career. The later textual level contains all the lines written in honor of the wedding allegorically celebrated and those bursts of verbal music that Shakespeare thought would charm the ladies and gentlemen of cultivated taste who would gather at the wedding celebration, and finally most of the lines dealing with the political satire and allegory half buried beneath the surface of the action.

The theme unifying the many strands of dramatic interest woven into the structure of *A Midsummer Night's Dream* is the ridiculous behavior of lovers of every sort and of every degree. Shakespeare's own opinion, at least as he presents it in the fantasy, is that love is a wholly irrational passion, the slave of whim and fancy. Theseus views its strange manifestations with tolerance, but Puck as an invitation to mischief.

1

Theseus and Hippolyta, having completed their rituals of courtship, are staid and serious, ready for marriage. They stand for the bride and groom for whose nuptials all the rest of the dramatic show has been prepared, presumably by Theseus' master of revels, Philostrate.

Theseus is no Greek tyrant but an English gentleman who, like Shakespeare, has his ears attuned to music of his hounds, in full cry (Act IV, Scene 1, lines 107–110):

> Go, one of you, find out the forester;
> For now our observation is performed;
> And since we have the vaward of the day,
> My love shall hear the music of my hounds.

(Act IV, Scene 1, lines 128–129):

> A cry more tuneable
> Was never holla'd to, nor cheered with horn

This passage is one of the poet's loving memories of his youth in Stratford that are scattered through the play.

Oberon's verses recited at the end of the play make it clear that the fantasy formed a part of a high-life wedding celebration. In these lines, Oberon dispatches a fairy minion to bless the marriage bed of all three couples, but especially the best bride-bed:

> To the best bride-bed will we,
> Which by us shall blessed be;
> And the issue there create
> Ever shall be fortunate.

Many weddings of the nobility have been suggested as the occasion of the acting of this comedy. One of the most likely is the marriage of the Earl of Derby with Elizabeth de Vere, the daughter of the Earl of Oxford, which was solemnized on January 26, 1595. A. L. Rowse, who sees the Earl of Southampton everywhere in Shakespeare's life and works, has recently nominated the Dowager Countess of Southampton, the mother of Shakespeare's patron and her third husband, Sir Thomas Heneage, as the principals in the real wedding that Shakespeare's play is celebrating. They were married on May 2, 1594. For this mature bride and groom, Oberon's verses are humorously inappropriate.

The comedy is an amalgam of three plots, the first of which is that of the four lovers. It is loosely connected with Theseus, the Duke of Athens, for it is to him that Egeus, the traditionally tyrannical father, appeals for aid in forcing his daughter Hermia to marry the youth of his choice. The poet's treatment of the game of cross purposes and mistaken identity is perfunctory. It is his development of the "errors" motif of Latin farce, the *Comedy of Errors*, and the complication of the Italianate love plot, a feature of both popular and learned comedy, with its two *amorosas* and two or three *amorosos*, which Shakespeare had already exploited in *The Two Gentlemen of Verona*. His lovers in this fantasy are mere pawns of the love-game played by the confused dramatis personae of the traditional plot. The poet's efforts to make the lovers' predicament seem real is superficially to differentiate them. Helena is the conventional lovelorn maiden of romance, the incarnation of external fidelity to the inconstant man. Her most characteristic exclamation is:

> I am your spaniel; and, Demetrius,
> The more you beat me, I will fawn on you.

Hermia is little, dark, and self-willed. She was accounted a vixen when she went to school, evidence that the girls went to a Petty school. Bitterly resenting Helena's flings at her small stature, she returns the taunts with interest, calling her a "painted Maypole." The explosions of her jealousy are so terrifying that Helena begs the men to protect her from Hermia's intended violence. The two *amorosos* are not so sharply distinguished. Demetrius is nearer the familiar type of sighing, rejected lover, Lysander being bolder and more resourceful. All four of them cherish the rites of romantic worship, the moonlight serenade, the exchange of bracelets of hair, of rings, of nosegays, and of candy. Love, to them, is an elaborate system of courtesy.

The poet must have introduced Puck and the fairies into the complications of the lovers at his first efforts to develop his initial story. Some of Oberon's and Puck's couplets are as mechanical and infelicitous as those in the exchange of the lovers, while others evoke magic more persuasively than any other verses that even Shakespeare ever wrote. They represent his final working over the manuscript.

The name Puck goes back to Anglo-Saxon times. Shakespeare had no need to learn about him from any treatise on English folk-lore. His head would have been stuffed with folk tales and nursery legends, like that of Puck and his pranks. Puck in this play is the official jester at the court of Oberon, king of the fairies. He explains that his business is to "jest to Oberon and make him smile." He also serves as the King's confidential messenger. He is clearly a tiny insubstantial elf,

like the other fairies. Near the end of the play, he once refers to himself as "we fairies" (Act V, Scene 1, line 390). In
all the legends, Puck is bent on mischief, delighted to confuse
and bewilder hapless mortals.

To this Ariel-like creature Shakespeare has given some of
the traits of Robin Goodfellow, a loutish rustic and friendly
sprite. One of Robin's good deeds is to enter the kitchen and
help with the housework in return for a bowl of cream and
a piece of bread set out on the kitchen doorstep for him. The
malicious tricks of which he boasts (Act II, Scene 1, lines 45–
57) are cruder and more farcical than those that Puck in his
own character displays. The other fairies, Peaseblossom, Cobweb, Moth, and Mustardseed, are almost wholly the figments
of the poet's imagination. They have been shorn of all that
was ill-natured and sinister in their originals in folklore to
become gay sprites, companion of moonbeams, and butterflies. They appear at midnight to dance in a ring or to break
into song at the slightest provocation. At sunrise they sud-
denly vanish. Such are the attendants of Oberon and Titania,
who under the name of Diana had been made queen of the
fairies by Elizabethan writers before Shakespeare, notably
Spenser and Lyly. These charming shapes which Shakespeare
has given to "airy nothing" are some of the most original
creations of his fancy. They lend the comedy an atmosphere
as fantastic and insubstantial as a dream of midsummer night
should be.

About his fairies the poet has woven that delicate charm
that Mendelssohn has translated into his famous incidental
music to the play. The magic is evoked partly by the fashion
in which Shakespeare has identified Oberon's realm with the
beauty of the English countryside when drenched in the

moonlight. Titania sleeps in a bower decked with the most beautiful of English flowers on

> a bank where the wild thyme blows,
> Where oxlips and the nodding violet grows,
> Quite over-canopied with luscious woodbine,
> With sweet musk-roses and with eglantine.

(Act II, Scene 1, lines 249–252).

Theseus describes the art by which his imagination gives to the airy nothing of this fairy world the local habitation of rural England as seen through a lover's eye. Shakespeare's poetic art by 1595 had become equal to this high and difficult task. His lyric impulse takes new and exquisite forms. The songs of Puck and the fairies are a perfect expression of the nature with which Shakespeare has endowed them. And the stately music in which Oberon and Titania carry on their quarrel over the "little changeling boy" has a depth and a richness of harmony new to English poetry.

Into this world of gossamerlike texture Bottom and his fellow artisans drop with a heavy thud. The performance of the "most lamentable comedy" is good-natured ridicule of the plays which the villagers in every part of England in Shakespeare's day used eagerly to produce. Among the entertainments offered Queen Elizabeth I when she went on a progress, there was almost certain to be a rustic show designed to provoke her mirth. The attempts of the folk of the village or countryside to present dramas dealing with classical or other elevated subjects must have been particularly ridiculous to sophisticated audiences. They found absurd, as do we, the bathetic language in which these plays were recited and the strange mixture of pseudo-heroic acting with the literal-minded realism which demanded that even Wall and Moonshine be impersonated by living men.

Bottom is the star of this troupe. Like all conceited amateur actors, he feels competent to impersonate any or all the characters in the tragedy. Though cast for the hero's role, he knows he could play the parts of the lady or the lion better than anyone else in the group—so versatile are his histrionic talents. But Shakespeare has given him a much fatter part in *A Midsummer Night's Dream* than any other of his low-comedy figures. Having designed the role for Will Kempe, the clown in his company and its most famous actor, Shakespeare expected Bottom to be, first of all, a lout. And lout he is, but one who completely transcends the traditional business of the character as we see it, for example, in Launce of *The Two Gentlemen of Verona*. He has progressed far beyond malapropism and rustic stupidity into a kind of folly that makes him an external comic embodiment of John Bull. Like that symbol of English stability, he is firmly rooted to the earth and feels completely at home in any spot on its broad surface. Nothing abashes him or disturbs his colossal self-assurance. Even his utterly strange experiences in fairyland do not give him a moment of astonishment or perplexity. When his head is laid in the lap of the fairy queen and she winds musk-roses in his hair, he feels no romantic fervor. He is merely conscious that his head itches and that it would be nice to have one of the doting Queen's tiny fairies scratch it. The lovely songs of these creatures of the other world do not destroy his preference for the good old tongs and bones. And the grossness which makes him utterly unable even to recognize anything unlike the round of his daily experiences rises to excellent dramatic farce in the scene in which he lays his long-eared ass's head on Titania's lap and falls complacently asleep upon her enamored bosom. Bottom through all his metamorphoses is one of the funniest characters in all dramatic literature, the first of Shakespeare's comic figures to maintain through every change of taste and literary fashion his irresistible appeal to the laughter of young and old, high and low. To every generation he is both a perfectly individualized clown and a persistent type of absurd human being.

All involved with the spell that the fairies weave and supporting the posturing of bully Bottom are hints of political and personal satire. They derive from the instructions Oberon gives Puck as he sends him forth to fetch a flower that maidens call love-in-idleness. The verses begin:

> My gentle Puck, come hither. Thou rememberest
> Since once I sat upon a promontory
> And heard a mermaid on a dolphin's back
> Uttering such dulcet and harmonious breath
> That the rude sea grew civil at her song
> And certain stars shot madly from their spheres,
> To hear the sea-maid's music.

These verses are a reminiscence of some gorgeous entertainment devised for the delight of Queen Elizabeth I and the ladies of her entourage when they visited some great lord's estate. Critics are now pretty well agreed that Oberon's references are to a water fete presented to his sovereign by the Earl of Hertford, at Elvetham, his country seat, in 1591.

The resemblances between the pageant and the occasion Oberon describes are close. A chart of the *mise en scène* of this fete contained in a contemporary pamphlet shows a promontory extending into an artificial, crescent-shaped lake. On its surface floats a boat, on the deck of which a mermaid is clearly to be discerned. The boat may have been really shaped like a dolphin, or perhaps it was the poet's imagination that so conceived it. The throne from which the Queen saw the operatic show and heard the water music appears to be on the western bank of the lake. The afternoon sun would have been at the Queen's back. So at Elvetham, Elizabeth was both imaginatively and literally "throned by the West." The "stars [that] shot madly from their spheres" are the fireworks that were a memorable feature of Hertford's show.

If Oberon is clearly referring to the Earl's lavish entertainment of the year 1591, why, in the year 1595, should he have wished to recall to the Queen the water fete with which he had regaled her four or five years before? The answer to this question is involved in a complicated tale of intrigue and royal tyranny.

It begins in 1560. In that year Hertford had secretly married Lady Catherine Grey, one of the Queen's ladies-in-waiting, or, as Titania says, "a votaress of my order" (i.e., of virginity). Elizabeth, pathologically jealous of any man or woman in her entourage who married without her permission, was particularly upset by Lady Catherine's wedlock, for she was descended from Henry VIII's sister, the Duchess of Suffolk. By the King's will, as well as by two acts of Parliament, any legitimate child of Lady Catherine stood next to Elizabeth in succession to the throne. So, when she gave birth to a son, the Queen threw her, and her husband, too, into prison. Then she contrived to have an Ecclesiastical Court declare the marriage null and void and the child illegitimate. In prison Lady Catherine, to the great annoyance of the Queen, proceeded to produce a second son. And in 1568 she, not "of that boy did die," as Titania says of the votaress, but did succumb to the cruel treatment she had received at the Queen's hands.

In 1580 the Earl began to protest against the findings of the Ecclesiastical Court, wishing particularly to have his sons made legitimate. His water fete of 1591 was part of his campaign to effect this result. In 1595 his machinations were discovered and their purpose to make his son the heir to the throne exposed. The infuriated Elizabeth immediately sent him to the Tower and held him there in peril of his life. At this time *A Midsummer Night's Dream* was presented.

If the play contains clear references to these events, the little changeling boy over whom Titania and Oberon quarrel is Hertford's son. Titania, or the Queen, would be the legal guardian of the child, although he should belong to Oberon's (King Henry VIII's) train because in his will he had designated him as his heir.

Some bold commentators suggest that Hertford expected the Queen to identify Oberon with Hertford himself. Was not the fairy land his creation? May not this fact give force and piquacy to Titania's answer to Oberon's pleading "The fairy land buys not the child of me"? (Act II, Scene 1, line 122). Your gorgeous water fete and your lavish expenditure in creating the fairy land at Elvetham are not impressive enough bribes to induce me to return your son to your care.

The intrusion of political and satiric meaning into what has long been known as a playful and merry fantasy has been violently repelled by many critics. Yet it explains so many features of the play which otherwise remain meaningless that much of this interpretation must be correct. The guests at a wedding in the highest Elizabethan society would expect some topical allusion in a play devised for their entertainment. The total absence of concealed meanings would have written down the author as rustically unfamiliar with the taste of the Queen and the sharp-witted ladies and gentlemen who followed in her train.

Besides these allusions to the situation of the Earl of Hertford, Shakespeare makes one very definite satiric personal reference to King James VI of Scotland. Quince, we remember, takes elaborate precautions to keep the ladies from being terrified at Snug's impersonation of a lion. In 1595 everyone at the English Court would laugh boisterously at such a reference, for it would call immediately to mind a recent revelation of the Scottish King's proverbial timidity. As a part of the festivities at the christening of his son Prince Henry at Sterling Castle on August 30, 1594, James had himself devised a pageant. At first he announced that a lion would draw in the baptismal car. But, becoming apprehensive about the danger to himself involved in such a plan, at the last moment he decided to substitute a Moor in the harness designed for the king of beasts, on the ground that a lion might frighten the ladies present at the ceremony out of their wits.

The indisputable piece of ridicule directed against King James led the late Miss Edith Rickert to search for other satiric allusions to that eccentric monarch and to find many clustering around the character of Bottom. The most entertaining of her discoveries explains how Bottom in the part of Pyramus might be a home thrust at King James, for in one of the monarch's poetic effusions he had likened himself to Pyramus. It happened in this way. Up to the year 1586 James hoped to marry his elder royal cousin Queen Elizabeth, and wooed her in poetical epistles. In one set of verses addressed to her, he reminds her that he and she are not like Hero and Leander separated by raging seas, but that their case is much more like that of Pyramus and Thisbe,

> Devyded onlie by a well,
>   Which in it had a bore,
> Where through they spake.

In the year 1594–1595, when *A Midsummer Night's Dream* was being composed, relations between the royal neighbors became very much strained. For at that time James was plotting with the Queen's enemies in the hope of securing the English throne for himself. Ridicule of him just then would have been popular at Elizabeth's court and his pretensions to the hand of the Queen and his awkward courtship food for laughter. However, the idea that Shakespeare designed Bottom as a ridiculous counterpart of James has seemed absurd to most critics. And the assumption that a dramatist, though writing only for an audience of courtiers, dared suggest to the Queen that if she refused to legitimatize Hertford's son, Fate might punish her by making her fall in love with her ridiculous cousin, they regard as preposterous.

Nevertheless it is improbable that so many detailed similarities between the two as Miss Rickert has found should be fortuitous. Robin Goodfellow's reiterated apologies for the dramatist in his final speech suggests that Shakespeare and the gentleman in whose interest he inserted the political and personal propaganda feared that they had been too bold in their satire. In its nervous anxiety, Robin's eagerness to explain away any offense the authors may have given to the courtly audience is like nothing else in Shakespeare. Its recurrent theme is

> Gentles, do not reprehend,
> If you pardon, we will mend.

Even if Shakespeare did give Bottom some of the characteristics of King James VI of Scotland, he never expected anyone in his audiences completely to identify the two. The methods of Elizabethan allegory and analogy were never so crass and obvious as that, and Shakespeare's subtle art much less so. He expected the gentle spectators in the know occasionally to discern a resemblance between the Scottish king and Bottom long enough to enjoy a burst of laughter. But after the quickest-minded had caught the fleeting likeness, Bottom would become entirely occupied with his own nature and for a long time be nothing but a fatuous weaver, round as a ball of wool, intent only upon giving a fine performance of Pyramus.

Many of Bottom's absurdities must have reminded Elizabeth of the peculiarities of her cousin-suitor over the border who had written a treatise entitled *Reulis* (ruler) *and Cantelis: Artifice to be Observit and Eschewit in Scottis Poesie.* In it he had particularly commended the figures of "repetition" and "alliteration," the two forms of rhetorical decoration to which Bottom was ridiculously addicted (cf. Act V, Scene 1, lines 147–148 and 171–178). And who but a Scotch Bottom would think of sending Mounsieur Cobweb for honey to a thistle?

Shakespeare's commission to write a play to be presented before the Queen herself at the country house of a great lord stimulated him to new artistic achievement. Never has he written passages of lovelier poetry. Never has he more successfully invoked natural magic. Never has he created a funnier low comedy figure than the asinine Bottom. The comedy marks one of the poet's most striking ascents on his way to the summit where his masterpieces shine in solitary glory.

Shakespeare's Life and Times

BY OSCAR JAMES CAMPBELL

We have little information about the private life of William Shakespeare. The facts enumerated in the following Chronology seldom reveal any secrets of the poet's personality or of his dramatic achievements. None of his associates in the theatre have left any record of their friend, whom they knew, respected, and admired. Nor did any of his contemporaries write even a brief account of his life. This is not strange. In sixteenth-century England only dignitaries of church or state were considered fit subjects for a biography.

The table below does make it clear that the poet was fortunate in the time of his birth, for, in the latter half of the sixteenth century, England basked in the full light of the Renaissance. He was equally fortunate in that the moment of his arrival on the scene coincided with new developments in the theatre. The first public playhouse was built in London when Shakespeare was in his early twenties. And when he began to write plays one company of actors had gained enough eminence and stability to provide a stage on which Shakespeare could bring to fruition all the elements of his genius.

The facts concerning his professional career, though more numerous, do not disclose any of the formative influences upon the design of the dramas or upon their distinctive character. However, these facts, joined with the meager records of the poet's personal life, have established the foundation upon which have been built all later biographies, interpretations, and criticisms of Shakespeare and his works.

Chronology

HISTORIC AND LITERARY EVENTS	SHAKESPEARE AND HIS FAMILY
1558 Elizabeth I crowned Queen. Thomas Kyd born. Robert Greene born.	
1561 Francis Bacon born.	John Shakespeare elected Chamberlain of Stratford.
1564 Christopher Marlowe born. Galileo Galilei born.	Shakespeare born, April 23; baptized, April 26.
1566	Gilbert, Shakespeare's brother, born; died 1612.
1567 Mary, Queen of Scots, dethroned. James VI (later James I of England) crowned.	
1572 Massacre of St. Bartholomew. Ben Jonson born.	
1573 John Donne born.	
1575 Earl of Leicester's entertainment of the Queen at Kenilworth.	

17

1576
Burbage builds the first public
    playhouse, The Theatre.

1577
Drake begins circumnavigation
    of the earth; finished 1580.
Holinshed's *Chronicles of
    England, Scotland, and
    Ireland.*

1579
John Lyly's *Euphues: The
    Anatomy of Wit.*

1581
Tenne Tragedies of Seneca.

1582

Marries Anne Hathaway.

1583
Philip Massinger born.   Shakespeare's daughter,
The Queen's Company formed.   Susanna, born.

1584
Reginald Scot's *The
    Discovery of Witchcraft.*

1585

Shakespeare's twins,
    Hamnet and Judith, born.

1586
Sir Philip Sidney killed at
    Zutphen.

John Ford born.

1587
Mary, Queen of Scots, beheaded.
Marlowe's *Tamburlaine, I.*
Kyd's *Spanish Tragedy.*

1588
Defeat of the Spanish Armada.
Principal actors of Lord
    Leicester's Company join
    Lord Strange's Men.
Marlowe's *Tamburlaine, II.*
Lyly's *Endimion.*

1589
Henry of Navarre crowned   *Comedy of Errors.*
    King of France as Henry IV.
Greene's *Friar Bacon and*
    Friar Bungay.
Marlowe's *Jew of Malta.*

1590
Sidney's *Arcadia.*   *Titus Andronicus.*
Spenser's *The Faerie Queene*   *Henry VI, I.*
    (I-III).

1591
                                  Henry VI, II.
                                  Henry VI, III.

1592
Death of Greene.   *Two Gentlemen of Verona.*
Marlowe's *Doctor Faustus* and
    Edward II.

1593
Theatres closed by plague.
Death of Marlowe.

Venus and Adonis.
Sonnets begun.
Richard III.

1594
Shakespeare's company becomes
  the Lord Chamberlain's Men.
Death of Kyd.

Rape of Lucrece.
Love's Labour's Lost.
Taming of the Shrew.
King John.

1595
Raleigh's first expedition to
  Guiana.
Spenser's *Amoretti,*
  Epithalamium.
Sidney's *Defense of Poesy*
  published.

Richard II.
A Midsummer Night's Dream.
Merchant of Venice.

1596
Spenser's *The Faerie Queene,*
  (*IV-VI*), *Four Hymns,* and
  Prothalamium.

Romeo and Juliet.
Hamnet Shakespeare dies.

1597
Bacon's *Essays* (first edition).
King James's *Demonologie.*

Henry IV, I.
Merry Wives of Windsor.
Shakespeare buys and renovates
  New Place in Stratford.

1598
Edict of Nantes issued by
  Henry IV, giving Huguenots
  political rights.
Jonson's *Every Man in His
  Humour* acted.
Seven books of Chapman's

Henry IV, II.
Much Ado About Nothing.

translation of the *Iliad*.

1599

Death of Spenser.	*Henry V.*
Globe Theatre built.	*Julius Caesar.*
Essex' expedition to Ireland.	
Jonson's *Every Man out of His Humour* acted.	
Dekker's *Shoemaker's Holiday*.	

1600

Fortune Theatre built.	*As You Like It.*
East India Company founded.	*Twelfth Night.*
Children of The Chapel acquire a hall in Blackfriars' Monastery.	

1601

Insurrection and execution of Essex.	*Hamlet.*
	Troilus and Cressida.

1602

Sir Thos. Bodley's Library at Oxford opened.	*All's Well That Ends Well.*

1603

Death of Queen Elizabeth I.
Accession of James I.
Shakespeare's company becomes the King's Men.
Heywood's *A Woman Killed with Kindness*.
Jonson's *Sejanus His Fall*.
Florio's translation of Montaigne's *Essays*.

1604
Treaty of Peace with Spain.

Measure for Measure.
Othello.

1605
The Gunpowder Plot.
Middleton's *A Trick to Catch the Old One.*

King Lear.

1606
Jonson's *Volpone.*

Macbeth.

1607
Settlement of Jamestown, Virginia.
Beaumont's *The Knight of the Burning Pestle.*

Antony and Cleopatra.
Timon of Athens.
Shakespeare's daughter Susanna married to Dr. John Hall.

1608
Burbage leases Blackfriars' Theatre for Shakespeare's company.
John Milton born.

Coriolanus.
Pericles, Prince of Tyre.

1609
Beaumont and Fletcher's *Philaster.*

Shakespeare's *Sonnets* published.

1610
Beaumont and Fletcher's *Maid's Tragedy.*

Cymbeline.

1611
Chapman completes translation of the *Iliad.*

The Winter's Tale.
The Tempest.

Authorized version of
  the Bible.

1612
Death of Prince Henry.
Beaumont retires from the
  theatre.
Webster's *The White Devil*.
Shelton's translation of
  Don Quixote, Part I.

1613
Globe Theatre burns.
Marriage of Princess Elizabeth
  to the Elector Palatine.

Henry VIII (with Fletcher).
The Two Noble Kinsmen (with
  Fletcher).
Buys a house in Blackfriars.

1614
Globe Theatre rebuilt.
Jonson's *Bartholomew Fair*.
Webster's *The Duchess of
  Malfi*.

1616
Death of Beaumont and
  Cervantes.
Jonson publishes his plays in a
  single volume entitled
  The Works of Ben Jonson.

Marriage of Judith Shakespeare
  to Thomas Quiney.
Death of Shakespeare, April 23.

1623
Publication of the Folio edition
  of Shakespeare's plays.

Death of Anne Hathaway.

Shakespeare's Theatre

BY STUART VAUGHAN

"The play in manuscript is only a blueprint for its performance in the theatre." This thought, whoever first gave voice to it, must have been one of Shakespeare's assumptions, for he took no care about the publishing of his work. He wrote plays to be acted, not to be read. These plays are as related to the theatre of Shakespeare's day as a shooting script is to modern film techniques. The structural evolution of that theatre, and the way it was used, profoundly influenced the nature of the plays themselves.

The simplest theatre of the Middle Ages was the platform of boards placed on trestles in the center of a town square. A frame at the back of the stage provided a place for the actors to be concealed, and from which to make their entrances. Sometimes the sides of the platform were curtained off so that the area under the stage could be used for dressing space. The platform was about five feet high in order that the audience standing around on three sides of the stage could see with fair comfort. In such simple surroundings, the text of the play had to tell the audience where the action was placed, and the actors themselves moved the few pieces of furniture in full view of the audience, since there was no provision for a front curtain, nor had anyone yet thought of that idea. Here already are the basic elements of Shakespeare's stage.

When, instead of passing the hat among the gathered audience, admission was charged to the enclosed yard of an inn, the other elements of the Elizabethan theatre had come together. Members of the audience still stood around the stage; but all about the circular courtyard more comfortable places were available—seats placed at the various windows and balconies of the inn, providing more ease and better visibility. In touring, James Burbage, the leading manager of the day, had made enough money to build a real theatre for plays. He had no precedent to follow but the shape of the inn yards he knew so well, and so he made his first building, The Theatre, in the circular shape which became the model for the subsequent public playhouses of this period.

Drawings and descriptions which have come down to us are not very definitive. Deductions from the plays themselves along with such contemporary information as we do possess have given us some notion of the form and use of this theatre. There were several tiers of galleries around the yard or "pit." These held the best places, and the occupants of these areas could sit and still see over the heads of the "groundlings" who gathered, standing in the pit, around the stage, which was still about five feet above ground level. The stage projected out into the pit, and was surrounded on at least three sides by audience. The galleries were roofed, and the stage was partially covered by a roof called "the shadow," but the standees in the pit were exposed to the open sky, which was the chief source of light for the plays. Performances took place at three in the afternoon.

There was some kind of permanent architectural background for the stage, with one large opening which revealed an area sometimes called "the inner stage." This opening was probably curtained, and most authorities conjecture that it was used for "discoveries," when the curtain could be drawn back to reveal a tableau, or a scene already set and in progress. It is doubtful that scenes of any length were played there, however, since, in order for the whole audience to see, the action would have been eventually brought down onto the projecting platform, or "forestage." There were at least two other doors, at the right and left of this large opening, which provided access to the stage. There was also an area above this main opening, probably some sort of gallery stretching along the back wall, where scenes could be played. Above that was a gallery for musicians.

Large properties, like beds or thrones, were probably discovered on the inner stage, but there was another means of moving furniture, dead bodies, or set pieces. "Mutes," or nonspeaking actors, were employed. They were probably masked and wore a conventional livery. They were the servants of the stage, and were either accepted as invisible by the audience, or functioned as servants, soldiers, or in similar capacities, carrying out necessary tasks like throne moving or wine pouring.

We are not sure what physical changes were made on the stage as the plays proceeded rapidly from, say, forest to castle to shipboard. We know that there were no intermissions or other interruptions in the performance. As actors for one scene left the stage, others for the next scene were already entering. Perhaps signs were hung denoting, for example, "The Boar's Head Tavern," but the dialogue is always so clear about change of locale that these seem hardly necessary.

Certainly most objects needed on the stage had to be of a portable nature. Certainly the pattern of physical action must have been in constant flux, like the turning of a wheel, to permit all members of the audience to see. The stage thus presented a continual flow of movement, not a series of static framed pictures.

The actors and the audience were in close contact. Indeed, certain noblemen were permitted to sit on the stage itself, apparently within arm's reach of the action. The actors' costumes were elaborate and expensive, to bear such close and sophisticated scrutiny, but to our eyes they would have presented a strange mixture of attempted historical accuracy and contemporary elegance. Shakespeare's theatre did not try to ignore the problem of presenting Romans who looked like Romans, but apparently neither actors nor public had a very clear idea of what Romans looked like.

We are dealing, then, with an active, exciting spectacle, presented on a very flexible stage which can stimulate the audience's imagination. We go into a movie theatre and are transported by two-dimensional images flashed on a silvered fabric. The Elizabethan audience watched and listened around a wooden platform where as great a transformation was possible through the mind's activity.

The truly complete production of Shakespeare today should permit the same speed of presentation, the same kind of physical action, the same actor-audience intimacy, and a similar imaginative participation on the part of the audience. In the last century elaborate scenic productions became the rule, but great waits for scene changes and large theatres demanding slow elocution necessitated vastly cut versions of the plays. The modern theatre has tried various means of getting back to Shakespeare. The "space stage" technique involves a stage bare of all but steps and platforms. Flexible lighting is relied on for change of locale and emphasis. The "unit set" provides basic walls and other pieces which, by means of simple and rapid adjustments, can be converted into a somewhat differently shaped acting area for each of a number of scenes. Revolving stages change more realistic scenery rapidly. Structural stages have been built which provide simple doors and platforms, giving us Shakespeare's acting space without his décor. Reconstructions of Elizabethan stages have been built and used. Various combinations of all these methods have been tried. Each director will make his own personal choice of method in realizing the particular play he is working on. If he is doing his job well, he will be in search of the best way he can to achieve his author's impact and intention with the means at his disposal in today's theatre.

A Midsummer Night's Dream

CHARACTERS

THESEUS, *duke of Athens.*

EGEUS, *father of Hermia.*

LYSANDER } *in love with*
DEMETRIUS } *Hermia.*

PHILOSTRATE, *master of the revels to Theseus.*

QUINCE, *a carpenter.*

SNUG, *a joiner.*

BOTTOM, *a weaver.*

FLUTE, *a bellows-mender.*

SNOUT, *a tinker.*

STARVELING, *a tailor.*

HIPPOLYTA, *queen of the Amazons, betrothed to Theseus.*

HERMIA, *daughter of Egeus, in love with Lysander.*

HELENA, *in love with Demetrius.*

OBERON, *king of the fairies.*

TITANIA, *queen of the fairies.*

PUCK, *or Robin Goodfellow.*

PEASEBLOSSOM
COBWEB
MOTH } *fairies.*
MUSTARDSEED

Other FAIRIES *attending their king and queen.* ATTENDANTS *on Theseus and Hippolyta.*

SCENE: Athens, and a wood near it.

ACT I

Scene 1. Athens. A hall in the palace of THESEUS.

(THESEUS *enters with* HIPPOLYTA, *followed by* PHILOSTRATE *and some* ATTENDANTS.)

THESEUS.

Now, fair Hippolyta, our nuptial hour
Draws on apace.[1] Four happy days bring in
Another moon: but, O, methinks, how slow
This old moon wanes! She lingers my desires,
Like to a step-dame* or a dowager   stepmother
Long withering out a young man's revenue.

HIPPOLYTA.

Four days will quickly steep themselves in night;
Four nights will quickly dream away the time;
And then the moon, like to a silver bow
New-bent in heaven, shall behold the night   10
Of our solemnities.

THESEUS.   Go, Philostrate,
Stir up the Athenian youth to merriments;
Awake the pert and nimble spirit of mirth.
Turn melancholy forth to funerals:

[1] See Notes, pp. 206 ff.

The pale companion is not for our pomp.
  (PHILOSTRATE *goes.*)
Hippolyta, I wooed thee with my sword,
And won thy love, doing thee injuries;
But I will wed thee in another key,
With pomp, with triumph,* and with reveling.   public show
    (EGEUS *enters, with* HERMIA, LYSANDER, *and*
  DEMETRIUS.)

EGEUS.

Happy be Theseus, our renownèd duke!   20

THESEUS.

Thanks, good Egeus. What's the news with thee?

EGEUS.

Full of vexation come I, with complaint
Against my child, my daughter Hermia.
  (*To* DEMETRIUS.)
Stand forth, Demetrius.
  (DEMETRIUS *steps forward.*)
                        My noble lord,
This man hath my consent to marry her.
Stand forth, Lysander.
  (LYSANDER *steps forward.*)
                        And, my gracious duke,
This man hath bewitched the bosom of my child.
Thou, thou, Lysander, thou hast given her rhymes
And interchanged love-tokens with my child:
Thou hast by moonlight at her window sung   30
With feigning* voice verses of feigning love,   dis-
                                                    sembling

And stolen the impression of her fantasy²
With bracelets of thy hair, rings, gawds,* conceits,*   trinkets/
                                                         love tokens
Knacks, trifles, nosegays, sweetmeats, messengers
Of strong prevailment in unhardened youth:
With cunning hast thou filched my daughter's
    heart,
Turned her obedience, which is due to me,
To stubborn harshness.
        (*To* THESEUS.)
                        And, my gracious duke,
Be it so she will not here before your grace
Consent to marry with Demetrius,   **40**
I beg the ancient privilege of Athens,
As she is mine, I may dispose of her.
Which shall be either to this gentleman
Or to her death, according to our law
Immediately* provided in that case.   expressly

THESEUS.

What say you, Hermia? Be advised, fair maid:
To you your father should be as a god;
One that composed your beauties, yea, and one
To whom you are but as a form in wax
By him imprinted and within his power   **50**
To leave the figure or disfigure* it.   obliterate
Demetrius is a worthy gentleman.

HERMIA.

So is Lysander.

THESEUS.   In himself he is;

But in this kind, wanting your father's voice,*   *i.e., of approval

The other must be held the worthier.

HERMIA.

I would my father looked but with my eyes.

THESEUS.

Rather your eyes must with his judgment look.

HERMIA.

I do entreat your grace to pardon me.

I know not by what power I am made bold,

Nor how it may concern my modesty,   60

In such a presence here to plead my thoughts;

But I beseech your grace that I may know

The worst that may befall me in this case,

If I refuse to wed Demetrius.

THESEUS.

Either to die the death or to abjure

Forever the society of men.

Therefore, fair Hermia, question your desires;

Know of your youth, examine well your blood,

Whether, if you yield not to your father's choice,

You can endure the livery of a nun,   70

For aye to be in shady cloister mewed,*   shut up

To live a barren sister all your life,

Chanting faint hymns to the cold fruitless moon.³

Thrice-blessèd they that master so their blood,*   passion

To undergo such maiden pilgrimage;

But earthlier happy is the rose distilled,

Than that which withering on the virgin thorn
Grows, lives, and dies in single blessedness.

HERMIA.

So will I grow, so live, so die, my lord,
Ere I will yield my virgin patent* up   privilege
Unto his lordship, whose unwished yoke   81
My soul consents not to give sovereignty.

THESEUS.

Take time to pause; and, by the next new moon—
The sealing-day betwixt my love and me,
For everlasting bond of fellowship—
Upon that day either prepare to die
For disobedience to your father's will,
Or else to wed Demetrius, as he would;
Or on Diana's altar to protest*   VOW
For aye austerity and single life.⁴   90

DEMETRIUS.

Relent, sweet Hermia. And, Lysander, yield
Thy crazèd* title to my certain right.   unsound

LYSANDER.

You have her father's love, Demetrius.
Let me have Hermia's: do you marry him.

EGEUS.

Scornful Lysander! True, he hath my love,
And what is mine my love shall render him.
And she is mine, and all my right of her
I do estate unto* Demetrius.   settle upon

LYSANDER.

I am, my lord, as well derived* as he,   descended
As well possessed,* my love is more than his;   well-off
My fortunes every way as fairly ranked,   101
If not with vantage, as Demetrius';
And, which is more than all these boast can be,
I am beloved of beauteous Hermia.
Why should not I then prosecute my right?
Demetrius, I'll avouch it to his head,*   face
Made love to Nedar's daughter, Helena,
And won her soul; and she, sweet lady, dotes,
Devoutly dotes, dotes in idolatry,
Upon this spotted and inconstant man.   110

THESEUS.

I must confess that I have heard so* much,   as
And with Demetrius thought to have spoke thereof;
But, being over-full of self-affairs,
My mind did lose it. But, Demetrius, come;
And come, Egeus; you shall go with me,
I have some private schooling for you both.
For you, fair Hermia, look you arm yourself
To fit your fancies to your father's will,
Or else the law of Athens yields you up—
Which by no means we may extenuate—   120
To death, or to a vow of single life.
Come, my Hippolyta: what cheer, my love?
Demetrius and Egeus, go* along: come
I must employ you in some business

Against* our nuptial and confer with you   in prepara-
Of something nearly* that concerns yourselves.   tion of
                                       pressing

EGEUS.

With duty and desire we follow you.

(THESEUS *and* HIPPOLYTA *leave, followed by* EGEUS,
DEMETRIUS, *and* ATTENDANTS.)

LYSANDER.

How now, my love! Why is your cheek so pale?
How chance the roses there do fade so fast?

HERMIA.

Belike for want of rain, which I could well   130
Beteem* them from the tempest of my eyes.   bring
                                     forth for

LYSANDER.

Ay me! For aught that I could ever read,
Could ever hear by tale or history,
The course of true love never did run smooth;
But, either it was different in blood—

HERMIA.

O cross! Too high to be enthralled to low.[5]

LYSANDER.

Or else misgraffèd* in respect of years—   ill-matched

HERMIA.

O spite! Too old to be engaged to young.

LYSANDER.

Or else it stood* upon the choice of friends—   depended

HERMIA.

O hell! To choose love by another's eyes.   140

LYSANDER.

Or, if there were a sympathy in choice,
War, death, or sickness did lay siege to it,
Making it momentany* as a sound,   momentary
Swift as a shadow, short as any dream,
Brief as the lightning in the collied* night,   coal-black
That, in a spleen,* unfolds both heaven and earth,   fit of anger
And ere a man hath power to say "Behold!"
The jaws of darkness do devour it up—
So quick bright things come to confusion.

HERMIA.

If then true lovers have been ever crossed,   150
It stands as an edìct in destiny.
Then let us teach our trial patience,
Because it is a customary cross,
As due to love as thoughts and dreams and sighs,
Wishes and tears, poor fancy's followers.

LYSANDER.

A good persuasion: therefore, hear me, Hermia.
I have a widow aunt, a dowager
Of great revènue, and she hath no child.
From Athens is her house remote seven leagues;
And she respects me as her only son.   160
There, gentle Hermia, may I marry thee;
And to that place the sharp Athenian law
Cannot pursue us. If thou lovest me then,
Steal forth thy father's house tomorrow night;
And in the wood, a league without the town,

Where I did meet thee once with Helena,
To do observance to* a morn of May,   celebrate
There will I stay for thee.

HERMIA.   My good Lysander!

I swear to thee, by Cupid's strongest bow,
By his best arrow with the golden head,   170
By the simplicity of Venus' doves,
By that which knitteth souls and prospers loves,
And by that fire which burned the Carthage queen,
When the false Troyan under sail was seen,[6]
By all the vows that ever men have broke,
In number more than ever women spoke,
In that same place thou hast appointed me,
Tomorrow truly will I meet with thee.

LYSANDER.

Keep promise, love.

                    Look, here comes Helena.

    (HELENA *enters.*)

HERMIA.

God speed fair Helena! Whither away?   180

HELENA.

Call you me fair? That fair again unsay.
Demetrius loves your fair:[7] O happy fair!*   fairness
Your eyes are lode-stars; and your tongue's
    sweet air
More tunable than lark to shepherd's ear,
When wheat is green, when hawthorn buds appear.

Sickness is catching: O, were favor* so,   features
Yours would I catch, fair Hermia, ere I go.
My ear should catch your voice, my eye your eye,
My tongue should catch your tongue's sweet 189
 melody.
Were the world mine, Demetrius being bated,* excepted
The rest I'd give to be to you translated.* transformed
O, teach me how you look, and with what art
You sway the motion of Demetrius' heart.

HERMIA.

I frown upon him, yet he loves me still.

HELENA.

O that your frowns would teach my smiles such
 skill!

HERMIA.

I give him curses, yet he gives me love.

HELENA.

O that my prayers could such affection move!

HERMIA.

The more I hate, the more he follows me.

HELENA.

The more I love, the more he hateth me.

HERMIA.

His folly, Helena, is no fault of mine.   200

HELENA.

None, but your beauty: would that fault were
 mine!

HERMIA.

Take comfort. He no more shall see my face:
Lysander and myself will fly this place.
Before the time I did Lysander see,
Seemed Athens as a paradise to me:
O, then, what graces in my love do dwell,
That he hath turned a heaven unto a hell!

LYSANDER.

Helen, to you our minds we will unfold:
Tomorrow night, when Phoebe doth behold
Her silver visage in the watery glass,[8]   210
Decking with liquid pearl the bladed grass,
A time that lovers' flights doth still conceal,
Through Athens' gates have we devised to steal.

HERMIA (*to* HELENA).

And in the wood, where often you and I
Upon faint* primrose-beds were wont to lie,   pale
Emptying our bosoms of their counsel sweet,
There my Lysander and myself shall meet;
And thence from Athens turn away our eyes,
To seek new friends and stranger companies.

   Farewell, sweet playfellow: pray thou for us;   220
And good luck grant thee thy Demetrius!
Keep word, Lysander: we must starve our sight
From lovers' food till morrow deep midnight.

LYSANDER.

I will, my Hermia.
   (HERMIA *leaves*). Helena, adieu.

As you on him, Demetrius dote on you!
    (LYSANDER *leaves.*)

HELENA.
    How happy some o'er other some can be!
    Through Athens I am thought as fair as she.
    But what of that? Demetrius thinks not so;
    He will not know what all but he do know:
    And as he errs, doting on Hermia's eyes,   **230**
    So I, admiring of his qualities.
    Things base and vile, holding no quantity,
    Love can transpose to form and dignity.
    Love looks not with the eyes, but with the mind;
    And therefore is winged Cupid painted blind.[9]
    Nor hath Love's mind of any judgment taste;
    Wings and no eyes figure* unheedy haste;   symbolize
    And therefore is Love said to be a child,
    Because in choice he is so oft beguiled.
    As waggish boys in game themselves forswear,   **240**
    So the boy Love is perjured everywhere;
    For ere Demetrius looked on Hermia's eyne,*   eyes
    He hailed down oaths that he was only mine;
    And when this hail some heat from Hermia felt,
    So he dissolved, and showers of oaths did melt.
      I will go tell him of fair Hermia's flight:
    Then to the wood will he tomorrow night
    Pursue her; and for this intelligence
    If I have thanks, it is a dear* expense;   costly
    But herein mean I to enrich my pain,   **250**

To have his sight thither and back again.
(HELENA *goes.*)

SCENE 2. A room in QUINCE's house in Athens.

(QUINCE, *the carpenter, enters; followed by* SNUG, *the joiner;* BOTTOM, *the weaver;* FLUTE, *the bellows-mender;* SNOUT, *the tinker; and* STARVELING, *the tailor.*)

QUINCE.
Is all our company here?

BOTTOM.
You were best to call them generally,*10 man by man, according to the scrip.*

i.e., separately script

QUINCE (*producing a scroll*).
Here is the scroll of every man's name, which is thought fit, through all Athens, to play in our interlude before the duke and the duchess, on his wedding-day at night.

BOTTOM.
First, good Peter Quince, say what the play treats on, then read the names of the actors and so grow to* a point.

arrive at/ **10**

QUINCE.
Marry, our play is "The most lamentable comedy, and most cruel death of Pyramus and Thisby."

BOTTOM.

A very good piece of work, I assure you, and a merry. Now, good Peter Quince, call forth your actors by the scroll. Masters, spread yourselves.

QUINCE.

Answer as I call you. (*Reading.*) Nick Bottom, the weaver.

BOTTOM.

Ready. Name what part I am for, and proceed. 20

QUINCE.

You, Nick Bottom, are set down for Pyramus.

BOTTOM.

What is Pyramus? A lover, or a tyrant?

QUINCE.

A lover, that kills himself most gallant for love.

BOTTOM.

That will ask some tears in the true performing of it. If I do it, let the audience look to their eyes; I will move storms, I will condole* in some meas- *i.e., lament* ure. To the rest. Yet my chief humor is for a ty- rant: I could play Ercles rarely, or a part to tear a 30 cat in, to make all split.[11]

> The raging rocks
> And shivering shocks
> Shall break the locks
>   Of prison gates;
> And Phibbus'* car   *i.e., Phoebus'*

Shall shine from far[12]
And make and mar
The foolish Fates.

40

This was lofty! Now name the rest of the players.
This is Ercles' vein, a tyrant's vein; a lover is more
condoling.

QUINCE (*reads*).
Francis Flute, the bellows-mender.

FLUTE.
Here, Peter Quince.

QUINCE.
Flute, you must take Thisby on you.

FLUTE.
What is Thisby? A wandering knight?

QUINCE.
It is the lady that Pyramus must love.

FLUTE.
Nay, faith, let not me play a woman; I have a
beard coming.

50

QUINCE.
That's all one. You shall play it in a mask, and
you may speak as small as you will.

BOTTOM.
An* I may hide my face, let me play Thisby too,
I'll speak in a monstrous little voice—"Thisne,
Thisne."*[13] "Ah Pyramus, my lover dear! Thy
Thisby dear, and lady dear!"

if

i.e.,
Thisbe

QUINCE.

No, no; you must play Pyramus; and, Flute, you
Thisby.

BOTTOM.

Well, proceed.

QUINCE (*reads*).

Robin Starveling, the tailor.   60

STARVELING.

Here, Peter Quince.

QUINCE.

Robin Starveling, you must play Thisby's mother.
(*Reads.*) Tom Snout, the tinker.

SNOUT.

Here, Peter Quince.

QUINCE.

You, Pyramus' father. Myself, Thisby's father.
(*Reads.*) Snug, the joiner, you the lion's part.
And, I hope, here is a play fitted.*   cast

SNUG.

Have you the lion's part written? Pray you, if it
be, give it me, for I am slow of study.

QUINCE.

You may do it extempore, for it is nothing but   70
roaring.

BOTTOM.

Let me play the lion too. I will roar, that I will
do any man's heart good to hear me; I will roar,

that I will make the duke say, "Let him roar again, let him roar again."

QUINCE.

An you should do it too terribly, you would fright the duchess and the ladies, that they would shriek; and that were enough to hang us all.

ALL.

That would hang us, every mother's son.   80

BOTTOM.

I grant you, friends, if that you should fright the ladies out of their wits, they would have no more discretion but to hang us; but I will aggravate* my voice so that I will roar you as gently as any suckling dove; I will roar you an* 'twere any nightingale.

i.e., moderate

as if

QUINCE.

You can play no part but Pyramus; for Pyramus is a sweet-faced man; a proper* man, as one shall see in a summer's day; a most lovely gentleman-like man: therefore you must needs play Pyramus.   90

handsome

BOTTOM.

Well, I will undertake it. What beard were I best to play it in?

QUINCE.

Why, what you will.

BOTTOM.

I will discharge it in either your straw-color beard,

your orange-tawny beard, your purple-in-grain*   deep red
beard, or your French-crown-color beard, your
perfect yellow.

QUINCE.

Some of your French crowns have no hair at all,
and then you will play barefaced. (*Hands out*   100
parts.) But, masters, here are your parts; and I am
to entreat you, request you, and desire you, to
con them* by tomorrow night, and meet me in the   know them by heart
palace wood, a mile without the town, by moon-
light; there will we rehearse, for if we meet in the
city, we shall be dogged with company, and our
devices* known. In the meantime I will draw a   plans
bill of properties, such as our play wants. I pray
you, fail me not.

BOTTOM.

We will meet; and there we may rehearse most   110
obscenely* and courageously. Take pains; be per-   *i.e.,* scene by scene
fect. Adieu.

QUINCE.

At the duke's oak we meet.

BOTTOM.

Enough; hold or cut bow-strings.[14]
   (*They all leave.*)

ACT II

Scene 1. Night. A wood near Athens.

(PUCK *and a* FAIRY *enter from opposite directions.*)

PUCK.
How now, spirit! Whither wander you?

FAIRY.
> Over hill, over dale,
>> Thorough* bush, thorough brier,
> Over park, over pale,*
>> Thorough flood, thorough fire,
> I do wander everywhere,
> Swifter than the moon's sphere;
> And I serve the fairy queen,
> To dew her orbs upon the green.[15]
> The cowslips tall her pensioners* be:[16]
> In their gold coats spots you see.
> Those be rubies, fairy favors,
> In those freckles live their savors.

through

fence

bodyguards

11

15, 16. See Notes, p. 209.

51

I must go seek some dewdrops here
And hang a pearl in every cowslip's ear.
  (*Starting to go.*)
Farewell, thou lob* of spirits. I'll be gone;   lout
Our queen and all her elves come here anon.

PUCK (*stopping the* FAIRY).

The king doth keep his revels here tonight:
Take heed the queen come not within his sight,
For Oberon is passing* fell* and wrath,   surpassingly/
                                      angry
Because that she as her attendant hath   21
A lovely boy, stolen from an Indian king.
She never had so sweet a changeling,[17]
And jealous Oberon would have the child
Knight of his train, to trace* the forests wild;   track
But she perforce withholds the lovèd boy,
Crowns him with flowers and makes him all her joy:
And now they never meet in grove or green,
By fountain clear, or spangled starlight sheen,
But they do square,* that all their elves for fear   quarrel
Creep into acorn-cups and hide them there.   31

FAIRY.

Either I mistake your shape and making quite,
Or else you are that shrewd* and knavish sprite   mischievous
Called Robin Goodfellow.[18] Are not you he
That frights the maidens of the villagery;
Skim milk, and sometimes labor in the quern*   hand mill
And bootless* make the breathless housewife churn; vainly
And sometime make the drink to bear no barm;*   foam

Mislead night-wanderers, laughing at their harm?
Those that Hobgoblin call you and sweet Puck,   40
You do their work, and they shall have good luck.
Are not you he?

PUCK.   Thou speak'st aright:
I am that merry wanderer of the night.
I jest to Oberon and make him smile
When I a fat and bean-fed horse beguile,
Neighing in likeness of a filly foal:
And sometime lurk I in a gossip's bowl,
In very likeness of a roasted crab,*   crabapple
And when she drinks, against her lips I bob
And on her withered dewlap pour the ale.   50
The wisest aunt,* telling the saddest tale,   *i.e.*, old woman
Sometime for three-foot stool mistaketh me;
Then slip I from her bum, down topples she,
And "Tailor" cries, and falls into a cough;[19]
And then the whole quire* hold their hips and   company
    laugh,
And waxen in their mirth and neeze* and swear   sneeze
A merrier hour was never wasted there.
    But, room, fairy! Here comes Oberon.

FAIRY (*moving aside*).
And here my mistress. Would that he were gone!
(*From opposite directions*, OBERON *and* TITANIA
*enter and face each other. Each is attended by a
train of* FAIRIES.)

OBERON.

Ill met by moonlight, proud Titania.   **60**

TITANIA.

What, jealous Oberon!
    (*To his train, as she starts to go.*)
                        Fairies, skip hence:
I have forsworn his bed and company.

OBERON (*stopping her*).

Tarry, rash wanton: am not I thy lord?

TITANIA.

Then I must be thy lady; but I know
When thou hast stolen away from fairy land,
And in the shape of Corin* sat all day,   *i.e., a*
                                                         shepherd
Playing on pipes of corn and versing love
To amorous Phillida.[20] Why art thou here,
Come from the farthest steppe of India
But that, forsooth, the bouncing Amazon,   **70**
Your buskined* mistress and your warrior love,   leather-
                                                         booted
To Theseus must be wedded, and you come
To give their bed joy and prosperity?

OBERON.

How canst thou thus for shame, Titania,
Glance at my credit with Hippolyta,
Knowing I know thy love to Theseus?
Didst thou not lead him through the glimmering
    night
From Perigenia, whom he ravished,

And make him with fair Aegle break his faith,
With Ariadne and Antiopa?[21]

TITANIA.

These are the forgeries of jealousy;
And never, since the middle summer's spring,*
Met we on hill, in dale, forest or mead,
By pavèd fountain or by rushy brook,
Or in the beachèd margent* of the sea,
To dance our ringlets to the whistling wind,
But with thy brawls thou hast disturbed our sport.
Therefore the winds, piping to us in vain,
As in revenge, have sucked up from the sea
Contagious fogs; which falling in the land
Have every pelting* river made so proud
That they have overborne their continents.*
The ox hath therefore stretched his yoke in vain,
The plowman lost his sweat, and the green corn
Hath rotted ere his youth attained a beard;
The fold stands empty in the drownèd field,
And crows are fatted with the murrion* flock;
The nine men's morris is filled up with mud,[22]
And the quaint* mazes in the wanton* green
For lack of tread are undistinguishable:
The human mortals want* their winter here;
No night is now with hymn or carol blest:
Therefore the moon, the governess of floods,
Pale in her anger, washes all the air,

90

paltry

banks

i.e., diseased

elaborate
lush
100

lack

That rhèumatic diseases do abound.
And thorough* this distemperature* we see   through/ disorder
The seasons alter: hoary-headed frosts
Fall in the fresh lap of the crimson rose,
And on old Hiems'* thin and icy crown   Winter's
An odorous chaplet of sweet summer buds   110
Is, as in mockery, set. The spring, the summer,
The childing* autumn, angry winter, change   fruitful
Their wonted liveries, and the mazèd* world,   amazed
By their increase, now knows not which is which.
And this same progeny of evils comes
From our debate, from our dissension:
We are their parents and original.*   origin

OBERON.

Do you amend it then; it lies in you.
Why should Titania cross her Oberon?
I do but beg a little changeling boy,   120
To be my henchman.*   page

TITANIA.   Set your heart at rest:
The fairy land buys not the child of me.
His mother was a votaress of my order;
And, in the spiced Indian air, by night,
Full often hath she gossiped by my side,
And sat with me on Neptune's yellow sands,
Marking the embarked traders* on the flood,   merchant ships
When we have laughed to see the sails conceive
And grow big-bellied with the wanton wind;

Which she, with pretty and with swimming gait   130
Following—her womb then rich with my young
    squire—
Would imitate, and sail upon the land,
To fetch me trifles, and return again,
As from a voyage, rich with merchandise.
But she, being mortal, of that boy did die;
And for her sake do I rear up her boy
And for her sake I will not part with him.

OBERON.

How long within this wood intend you stay?

TITANIA.

Perchance till after Theseus' wedding-day.
If you will patiently dance in our round   140
And see our moonlight revels, go with us;
If not, shun me, and I will spare* your haunts.   avoid

OBERON.

Give me that boy, and I will go with thee.

TITANIA.

Not for thy fairy kingdom. Fairies, away!
We shall chide downright, if I longer stay.
    (TITANIA *goes, followed by her train of* ATTEND-
    ANTS.)

OBERON.

Well, go thy way: thou shalt not from this grove
Till I torment thee for this injury.
    My gentle Puck, come hither. Thou rememberest

Since once I sat upon a promontory,
And heard a mermaid on a dolphin's back   **150**
Uttering such dulcet and harmonious breath
That the rude sea grew civil at her song
And certain stars shot madly from their spheres,
To hear the sea-maid's music.

PUCK.   I remember.

OBERON.

That very time I saw, but thou couldst not,
Flying between the cold moon and the earth,
Cupid all armed. A certain aim he took
At a fair vestal thronèd by the west,
And loosed his love-shaft smartly from his bow,
As* it should pierce a hundred thousand hearts;   **as if/160**
But I might see young Cupid's fiery shaft
Quenched in the chaste beams of the watery moon,
And the imperial votaress passed on,23
In maiden meditation, fancy-free.
Yet marked I where the bolt of Cupid fell:24
It fell upon a little western flower,
Before milk-white, now purple with love's wound,
And maidens call it love-in-idleness.*25   **pansy**
Fetch me that flower; the herb I showed thee once.
The juice of it on sleeping eyelids laid   **170**
Will make or man or woman madly dote
Upon the next live creature that it sees.
Fetch me this herb; and be thou here again
Ere the leviathan* can swim a league.   ***i.e.,* whale**

PUCK.

> I'll put a girdle round about the earth
> In forty minutes.
>   (PUCK *goes*.)

OBERON.   Having once this juice,

> I'll watch Titania when she is asleep,
> And drop the liquor of it in her eyes.
> The next thing then she waking looks upon,
> Be it on lion, bear, or wolf, or bull,   180
> On meddling monkey, or on busy ape,
> She shall pursue it with the soul of love.
> And ere I take this charm from off her sight,
> As I can take it with another herb,
> I'll make her render up her page to me.
>   But who comes here? I am invisible;
> And I will overhear their conference.
>   (*As* OBERON *steps aside*, DEMETRIUS *enters, fol-
>   lowed by* HELENA.)

DEMETRIUS.

> I love thee not, therefore pursue me not.
> Where is Lysander and fair Hermia?
> The one I'll slay, the other slayeth me.   190
> Thou told'st me they were stolen unto this wood;
> And here am I, and wode* within this wood,   mad
> Because I cannot meet my Hermia.
> Hence, get thee gone, and follow me no more.

HELENA.

You draw me, you hard-hearted adamant;*   magnet
But yet you draw not iron, for my heart
Is true as steel. Leave you* your power to draw,   give up
And I shall have no power to follow you.

DEMETRIUS.

Do I entice you? Do I speak you fair?
Or, rather, do I not in plainest truth   200
Tell you, I do not, nor I cannot love you?

HELENA.

And even for that do I love you the more.
I am your spaniel; and, Demetrius,
The more you beat me, I will fawn on you.
Use me but as your spaniel, spurn me, strike me,
Neglect me, lose me—only give me leave,
Unworthy as I am, to follow you.
What worser place can I beg in your love—
And yet a place of high respect with me—
Than to be usèd as you use your dog?   210

DEMETRIUS.

Tempt not too much the hatred of my spirit,
For I am sick when I do look on thee.

HELENA.

And I am sick when I look not on you.

DEMETRIUS.

You do impeach* your modesty too much,   endanger
To leave the city and commit yourself
Into the hands of one that loves you not;

To trust the opportunity of night
And the ill counsel of a desert place
With the rich worth of your virginity.

HELENA.

Your virtue is my privilege:* for that   protection
It is not night when I do see your face,   221
Therefore I think I am not in the night;
Nor doth this wood lack worlds of company,
For you in my respect* are all the world.   regard
Then how can it be said I am alone,
When all the world is here to look on me?

DEMETRIUS.

I'll run from thee and hide me in the brakes,*   thickets
And leave thee to the mercy of wild beasts.

HELENA.

The wildest hath not such a heart as you.
Run when you will, the story shall be changed: 230
Apollo flies, and Daphne holds the chase;[26]
The dove pursues the griffin;[27] the mild hind
Makes speed to catch the tiger. Bootless speed,
When cowardice pursues and valor flies.

DEMETRIUS.

I will not stay thy question;* let me go;   for thy talk
Or, if thou follow me, do not believe
But I shall do thee mischief in the wood.

HELENA.

Ay, in the temple, in the town, the field,
You do me mischief. Fie, Demetrius!

Your wrongs do set a scandal on my sex.   **240**
We cannot fight for love, as men may do;
We should be wooed and were not made to woo.
    (DEMETRIUS *leaves.*)
I'll follow thee and make a heaven of hell,
To die* upon the hand I love so well.   by dying
    (HELENA *follows him.*)
OBERON.
Fare thee well, nymph: ere he do leave this grove,
Thou shalt fly him and he shall seek thy love.
    (PUCK *returns.*)
Hast thou the flower there? Welcome, wanderer.
PUCK (*revealing the flower*).
Ay, there it is.
OBERON.   I pray thee, give it me.
    (*Taking the flower.*)
I know a bank where the wild thyme blows,*   blooms
Where oxlips and the nodding violet grows,   **250**
Quite over-canopied with luscious woodbine,
With sweet musk-roses and with eglantine.
There sleeps Titania sometime of the night,
Lulled in these flowers with dances and delight;
And there the snake throws* her enameled skin,   sheds
Weed* wide enough to wrap a fairy in.   garment
And with the juice of this I'll streak* her eyes,   touch
And make her full of hateful fantasies.
    (*Handing* PUCK *a portion of the flower.*)
Take thou some of it, and seek through this grove:

A sweet Athenian lady is in love
With a disdainful youth. Anoint his eyes—
But do it when the next thing he espies
May be the lady. Thou shalt know the man
By the Athenian garments he hath on.
Effect it with some care that he may prove
More fond on her than she upon her love.
And look thou meet me ere the first cock crow.

PUCK.

Fear not, my lord, your servant shall do so.

(PUCK *leaves.*)

SCENE 2. Another part of the wood.

(TITANIA *enters, followed by her train of attendant* FAIRIES.)

TITANIA.

Come, now a roundel* and a fairy song;   round-dance
Then, for the third part of a minute, hence;
Some to kill cankers* in the musk-rose buds,   worms
Some war with rere-mice* for their leathern wings   bats
To make my small elves coats; and some keep back
The clamorous owl that nightly hoots and wonders
At our quaint spirits.

(*Lying down in a bower.*)

Sing me now asleep;
Then to your offices* and let me rest.   duties
(*The* FAIRIES *sing.*)

You spotted snakes with double tongue,
   Thorny hedgehogs, be not seen;   **10**
Newts and blind-worms,* do no wrong,   lizards
   Come not near our fairy queen.
   Philomel,* with melody   *i.e.,* nightingale
   Sing in our sweet lullaby;[28]
Lulla, lulla, lullaby, lulla, lulla, lullaby;
   Never harm,
   Nor spell nor charm,
Come our lovely lady nigh.
So, good night, with lullaby.

Weaving spiders, come not here;   **20**
   Hence, you long-legged spinners, hence!
Beetles black, approach not near;
   Worm nor snail, do no offense.
   Philomel, with melody
   Sing in our sweet lullaby;
Lulla, lulla, lullaby, lulla, lulla, lullaby;
   Never harm,
   Nor spell nor charm,
Come our lovely lady nigh.
So, good night, with lullaby.

A FAIRY.
Hence, away! Now all is well:

One aloof stand sentinel.

(TITANIA *falls asleep and the* FAIRIES *slip away. After a moment,* OBERON *enters and squeezes juice from the flower on* TITANIA'*s eyelids.*)

OBERON.

What thou seest when thou dost wake,
Do it for thy true-love take,
Love and languish for his sake:
Be it ounce,* or cat,* or bear,
Pard,* or boar with bristled hair,
In thy eye that shall appear
When thou wakest, it is thy dear:
Wake when some vile thing is near.

lynx/
wildcat/30
leopard

(OBERON *goes.* TITANIA *sleeps on, concealed in her bower of leaves and flowers. After a moment,* LYSANDER *and* HERMIA *enter.*)

LYSANDER.

Fair love, you faint with wandering in the wood;
And to speak troth,* I have forgot our way.
We'll rest us, Hermia, if you think it good,
And tarry for the comfort of the day.

truth

HERMIA (*sinking down onto the grass*).

Be it so, Lysander. Find you out a bed;
For I upon this bank will rest my head.

40

LYSANDER (*lying down beside her*).

One turf shall serve as pillow for us both;
One heart, one bed, two bosoms, and one troth.*

i.e., plighted
troth

HERMIA.

Nay, good Lysander; for my sake, my dear,
Lie further off yet, do not lie so near.

LYSANDER.

O, take the sense, sweet, of my innocence!
Love takes the meaning in love's conference.
I mean, that my heart unto yours is knit
So that but one heart we can make of it;
Two bosoms interchainèd with an oath;
So then two bosoms and a single troth.   50
Then by your side no bed-room me deny;
For lying so, Hermia, I do not lie.

HERMIA.

Lysander riddles very prettily:
Now much beshrew* my manners and my pride,   fie upon
If Hermia meant to say Lysander lied.
But, gentle friend, for love and courtesy
Lie further off; in human* modesty,   decorous
Such separation as may well be said
Becomes a virtuous bachelor and a maid,
So far be distant.
    (LYSANDER *rises.*)
              And, good night, sweet friend: 60
Thy love ne'er alter till thy sweet life end!

LYSANDER (*moving some distance away*).

Amen, amen, to that fair prayer, say I;
And then end life when I end loyalty!
    (*Lying down.*)

Here is my bed: sleep give thee all his rest!

HERMIA.

With half that wish the wisher's eyes be pressed!

(LYSANDER *and* HERMIA *fall asleep. After a moment,* PUCK *enters.*)

PUCK.

Through the forest have I gone,
But Athenian found I none,
On whose eyes I might approve*   prove
This flower's force in stirring love.
Night and silence.

(*Seeing* LYSANDER *and* HERMIA.)

Who is here?   **70**
Weeds* of Athens he doth wear;   garments
This is he, my master said,
Despised the Athenian maid;
And here the maiden, sleeping sound,
On the dank and dirty ground.
Pretty soul! She durst not lie
Near this lack-love, this kill-courtesy.

(*Squeezing juice from the flower on* LYSANDER's
eyelids.)

Churl, upon thy eyes I throw
All the power this charm doth owe.*   own
When thou wakest, let love forbid   **80**
Sleep his seat on thy eyelid:
So awake when I am gone;

    For I must now to Oberon.

    (PUCK *leaves. A moment later,* DEMETRIUS *runs in followed by* HELENA.)

HELENA.

Stay, though thou kill me, sweet Demetrius.

DEMETRIUS.

I charge thee, hence, and do not haunt me thus.

HELENA.

O, wilt thou darkling* leave me? Do not so.   in the dark

DEMETRIUS.

Stay, on thy peril. I alone will go.

    (DEMETRIUS *leaves.*)

HELENA.

I am out of breath in this fond* chase!   foolish

The more my prayer, the lesser is my grace.

Happy is Hermia, wheresoe'er she lies;   90

For she hath blessèd and attractive eyes.

How came her eyes so bright? Not with salt tears:

If so, my eyes are oftener washed than hers.

No, no, I am as ugly as a bear;

For beasts that meet me run away for fear.

Therefore no marvel though Demetrius

Do, as a monster, fly my presence thus.

What wicked and dissembling glass of mine

Made me compare with Hermia's sphery eyne?*   starry eyes

    (*Discovering* LYSANDER.)

But who is here? Lysander! On the ground!   100

Dead? Or asleep? I see no blood, no wound.

(*Shaking him.*)
Lysander, if you live, good sir, awake.

LYSANDER (*awaking*).

And run through fire I will for thy sweet sake.
Transparent Helena! Nature shows art,
That through thy bosom makes me see thy heart.
Where is Demetrius? O, how fit a word
Is that vile name to perish on my sword!

HELENA.

Do not say so, Lysander; say not so.
What though he love your Hermia? Lord, what
   though?
Yet Hermia still loves you: then be content.   **110**

LYSANDER.

Content with Hermia! No; I do repent
The tedious minutes I with her have spent.
Not Hermia but Helena I love:
Who will not change a raven for a dove?
The will of man is by his reason swayed;
And reason says you are the worthier maid.
Things growing are not ripe until their season
So I, being young, till now ripe not* to reason;   not ripe
And touching now the point* of human skill,   summit
Reason becomes the marshal to my will   **120**
And leads me to your eyes, where I o'erlook
Love's stories written in love's richest book.

HELENA.

Wherefore was I to this keen mockery born?

When at your hands did I deserve this scorn?
Is 't not enough, is 't not enough, young man,
That I did never, no, nor never can,
Deserve a sweet look from Demetrius' eye,
But you must flout my insufficiency?
Good troth, you do me wrong, good sooth, you do,
In such disdainful manner me to woo.   130
But fare you well: perforce I must confess
I thought you lord of more true gentleness.
O, that a lady, of one man refused,
Should of another therefore be abused!

    (HELENA *leaves.*)

LYSANDER.

She sees not Hermia. Hermia, sleep thou there:
And never mayst thou come Lysander near!
For as a surfeit of the sweetest things
The deepest loathing to the stomach brings,
Or as the heresies that men do leave
Are hated most of those they did deceive,   140
So thou, my surfeit and my heresy,
Of all be hated, but the most of me!
And, all my powers, address your love and might
To honor Helen and to be her knight!

    (LYSANDER *hurries off after* HELENA. *After a moment,* HERMIA *wakes up.*)

HERMIA.

Help me, Lysander, help me! Do thy best
To pluck this crawling serpent from my breast!

Ay me, for pity! What a dream was here!
Lysander, look how I do quake with fear:
Methought a serpent eat my heart away,
And you sat smiling at his cruel prey.*

149
preying

    (*Discovering* LYSANDER'*s absence*.)
Lysander! What, removed? Lysander! Lord!
What, out of hearing? Gone? No sound, no word?
Alack, where are you? Speak, an if you hear;
Speak, of* all loves! I swoon almost with fear.

for the
sake of

No? Then I well perceive you are not nigh:
Either death or you I'll find immediately.

    (HERMIA *leaves*.)

ACT III

Scene 1. The same spot in the wood.

(TITANIA *is still asleep in her bower.* QUINCE *enters, followed by* SNUG, BOTTOM, FLUTE, SNOUT *and* STARVELING.)

BOTTOM.

Are we all met?

QUINCE.

Pat, pat; and here's a marvelous convenient place for our rehearsal. This green plot shall be our stage, this hawthorn brake our tiring-house;* and we will do it in action as we will do it before the duke.

dressing room

BOTTOM.

Peter Quince—

QUINCE.

What sayest thou, bully* Bottom?

good fellow

BOTTOM.

There are things in this comedy of Pyramus and Thisby that will never please. First, Pyramus must draw a sword to kill himself; which the ladies can-

10

not abide. How answer you that?

SNOUT.

By 'r lakin,* a parlous* fear.

by our lady/
perilous

STARVELING.

I believe we must leave the killing out, when all is done.

BOTTOM.

Not a whit: I have a device to make all well. Write me a prologue; and let the prologue seem to say, we will do no harm with our swords and that Pyramus is not killed indeed; and, for the more better assurance, tell them that I Pyramus am not Pyramus, but Bottom the weaver. This will put them out of fear.

20

QUINCE.

Well, we will have such a prologue; and it shall be written in eight and six.[29]

BOTTOM.

No, make it two more; let it be written in eight and eight.

SNOUT.

Will not the ladies be afeard of the lion?

STARVELING.

I fear it, I promise you.

BOTTOM.

Masters, you ought to consider with yourselves: to bring in—God shield us!—a lion among ladies, is a most dreadful thing; for there is not a more fear-

30

ful wild-fowl than your lion living; and we ought to look to 't.

SNOUT.

Therefore another prologue must tell he is not a lion.

BOTTOM.

Nay, you must name his name, and half his face must be seen through the lion's neck: and he himself must speak through, saying thus, or to the same defect—"Ladies"— or "Fair ladies—I would wish you"—or "I would request you"—or "I would entreat you—not to fear, not to tremble. My life for yours. If you think I come hither as a lion, it were pity of* my life. No, I am no such thing: I am a man as other men are"; and there indeed let him name his name, and tell them plainly he is Snug the joiner. 40

*danger for

QUINCE.

Well, it shall be so. But there is two hard things; that is, to bring the moonlight into a chamber; for, you know, Pyramus and Thisby meet by moonlight. 50

SNOUT.

Doth the moon shine that night we play our play?

BOTTOM.

A calendar, a calendar! Look in the almanac; find out moonshine, find out moonshine.

QUINCE (*after looking in the almanac*).

Yes, it doth shine that night.

BOTTOM.

Why, then may you leave a casement of the great chamber window, where we play, open, and the moon may shine in at the casement. Hi the

QUINCE.

Ay; or else one must come in with a bush of thorns and a lanthorn,*[30] and say he comes to disfigure, or to present,* the person of Moonshine. Then, there is another thing: we must have a wall in the great chamber; for Pyramus and Thisby, says the story, did talk through the chink of a wall.

60

lantern

i.e.,
model or
represent

SNOUT.

You can never bring in a wall. What say you, Bottom?

BOTTOM.

Some man or other must present Wall. And let him have some plaster, or some loam, or some rough-cast* about him, to signify wall; and let him hold his fingers thus, and through that cranny shall Pyramus and Thisby whisper.

70

coarse
plaster

QUINCE.

If that may be, then all is well. Come, sit down, every mother's son, and rehearse your parts. Pyramus, you begin: when you have spoken your speech, enter into that brake:* and so everyone

thicket

according to his cue.

(*As the men move into position to begin rehearsals,* PUCK *enters behind them.*)

PUCK.

What hempen home-spuns have we swaggering
  here,
So near the cradle of the fairy queen?   **80**
    What, a play toward!* I'll be an auditor;   *i.e., in*
An actor too perhaps, if I see cause.   **preparation**

QUINCE (*following the script*).

Speak, Pyramus. Thisby, stand forth.

BOTTOM.

Thisby, the flowers of odious savors sweet—

QUINCE.

Odors, odors.

BOTTOM.

—odors savors sweet:
So hath thy breath, my dearest Thisby dear.
But hark, a voice! Stay thou but here awhile,
And by and by* I will to thee appear. *with that* **at once**
    (BOTTOM *goes.*) *He Died.*

PUCK.

A stranger Pyramus than e'er played here.   **90**
    (PUCK *follows* BOTTOM.)

FLUTE.

Must I speak now?

QUINCE.

Ay, marry, must you; for you must understand he

goes but to see a noise that he heard, and is to come again.

FLUTE.

Most radiant Pyramus, most lily-white of hue,
Of color like the red rose on triumphant brier,
Most brisky juvenal* and eke* most lovely Jew,[31]   juvenile/
                                                         also
As true as truest horse that yet would never tire,
I'll meet thee, Pyramus, at Ninny's tomb.[32]

QUINCE.

"Ninus' tomb," man. Why, you must not speak   100
that yet; that you answer to Pyramus: you speak
all your part at once, cues and all. Pyramus enter.
Your cue is past: it is "Never tire."

FLUTE.

O—As true as truest horse, that yet would never
    tire.
    (BOTTOM *enters. His head has been changed to
    that of a donkey but he is not aware of it. He is
    followed by* PUCK, *who is invisible to the other
    characters.*)

BOTTOM.

If I were fair, Thisby, I were only thine. But NO

QUINCE.

O monstrous! O strange! We are haunted. Pray,
masters! Fly, masters! Help!
    (QUINCE, SNUG, FLUTE, SNOUT, *and* STARVELING *all
    run away.*)

PUCK.

I'll follow you, I'll lead you about a round,*   round about

Through bog, through bush, through brake,
    through brier.   110

Sometimes a horse I'll be, sometime a hound,

    A hog, a headless bear, sometime a fire;

And neigh, and bark, and grunt, and roar, and
    burn,

Like a horse, hound, hog, bear, fire, at every turn.

    (PUCK *follows the men off*.)

BOTTOM.

Why do they run away? This is a knavery of
them to make me afeard.

    (SNOUT *returns*.)

SNOUT.

O Bottom, thou art changed! What do I see on
thee?

BOTTOM.

What do you see? You see an ass-head of your
own, do you?   120

    (SNOUT *goes, and* QUINCE *comes back*.)

QUINCE.

Bless thee, Bottom! Bless thee! Thou art translated.*   transformed

    (QUINCE *runs away*.)

BOTTOM.

I see their knavery: this is to make an ass of me;
to fright me, if they could. But I will not stir

from this place, do what they can. I will walk up
and down here, and I will sing, that they shall hear
I am not afraid. (*Sings.*)

> The ousel* cock so black of hue,   blackbird
>   With orange-tawny bill,
> The throstle* with his note so true,   thrush/130
>   The wren with little quill*—   pipe

TITANIA (*awakening within her bower*).
What angel wakes me from my flowery bed?

BOTTOM (*sings*).
> The finch, the sparrow and the lark,
>   The plain-song cuckoo gray,[33]
> Whose note full many a man doth mark,
>   And dares not answer nay—

for, indeed, who would set his wit to so foolish a
bird? Who would give a bird the lie, though he
cry "cuckoo" never so?

TITANIA (*emerging from her bower*).
I pray thee, gentle mortal, sing again: 140
Mine ear is much enamored of thy note;
So is mine eye enthrallèd to thy shape;
And thy fair virtue's* force perforce doth   beauty's
    move me
On the first view to say, to swear, I love thee.

BOTTOM.
Methinks, mistress, you should have little reason
for that: and yet, to say the truth, reason and love
keep little company together nowadays; the more

the pity that some honest neighbors will not make them friends. Nay, I can gleek* upon occasion.   scoff/150

TITANIA.

Thou art as wise as thou art beautiful.

BOTTOM.

Not so, neither: but if I had wit enough to get out of this wood, I have enough to serve mine own turn.

TITANIA.

Out of this wood do not desire to go.
Thou shalt remain here, whether thou wilt or no.
I am a spirit of no common rate,*   *I'm Queen spirit,*   rank
The summer still doth tend upon my state;* *I control*   court
                                            seasons
And I do love thee: therefore, go with me;
I'll give thee fairies to attend on thee,   160
And they shall fetch thee jewels from the deep,
And sing while thou on pressed flowers dost sleep.
And I will purge thy mortal grossness so   *I'll take away the bad stuff that comes w/ being a mortal.*
That thou shalt like an airy spirit go.
Peaseblossom! Cobweb! Moth! And Mustard-
    seed!

(PEASEBLOSSOM, COBWEB, MOTH, *and* MUSTARD-
    SEED *all appear.*)

PEASEBLOSSOM. Ready.

COBWEB.   And I.

MOTH.   And I.

MUSTARDSEED.   And I.

ALL.   Where shall we go?

TITANIA.

    Be kind and courteous to this gentleman;

    Hop in his walks and gambol in his eyes;

    Feed him with apricocks* and dewberries,   **apricots**

    With purple grapes, green figs, and mulberries;   **170**

    The honey-bags steal from the humble-bees,

    And for night-tapers crop* their waxen thighs   **trim**

    And light them at the fiery glow-worm's eyes,

    To have my love to bed and to arise;

    And pluck the wings from painted butterflies

    To fan the moonbeams from his sleeping eyes.

    Nod to him, elves, and do him courtesies.

PEASEBLOSSOM.

    Hail, mortal!

COBWEB.

    Hail!

MOTH.

    Hail!   **180**

MUSTARDSEED.

    Hail!

BOTTOM.

    I cry your worships mercy,* heartily. (*To another*   **pardon**
FAIRY.) I beseech your worship's name.

COBWEB.

    Cobweb.

BOTTOM.

    I shall desire you of more acquaintance, good
Master Cobweb: if I cut my finger, I shall make

bold with you. Your name, honest gentleman?

PEASEBLOSSOM.

Peaseblossom.

BOTTOM.

I pray you, commend me to Mistress Squash,* your mother, and to Master Peascod, your father. Good Master Peaseblossom, I shall desire you of more acquaintance too. Your name, I beseech you, sir?

unripe peapod 191

MUSTARDSEED.

Mustardseed.

BOTTOM.

Good Master Mustardseed, I know your patience* well: that same cowardly, giant-like ox-beef hath devoured many a gentleman of your house. I promise you your kindred hath made my eyes water ere now. I desire your more acquaintance, good Master Mustardseed.

courage

200

TITANIA.

Come, wait upon him; lead him to my bower.
  The moon methinks looks with a watery eye;
And when she weeps, weeps every little flower,
  Lamenting some enforcèd* chastity.
Tie up my love's tongue, bring him silently.
(*The* FAIRIES *wrap garlands around* BOTTOM *and lead him into the bower, followed by* TITANIA.)

violated

SCENE 2. Another part of the wood.

(OBERON *enters*).

OBERON.
I wonder if Titania be awaked;
Then, what it was that next came in her eye,
Which she must dote on in extremity.
    Here comes my messenger.
    (PUCK *enters*.)
                                    How now, mad spirit!
What night-rule* now about this haunted grove?   action

PUCK.
My mistress with a monster is in love.
Near to her close and consecrated bower,
While she was in her dull and sleeping hour,
A crew of patches,* rude mechanicals,*   dolts/
                                                        mechanics
That work for bread upon Athenian stalls,*   shops/10
Were met together to rehearse a play
Intended for great Theseus' nuptial-day.
The shallowest thick-skin of that barren sort,*   stupid lot
Who Pyramus presented, in their sport
Forsook his scene and entered in a brake,
When I did him at this advantage take:
An ass's nole* I fixèd on his head.   noddle
Anon his Thisbe must be answered,
And forth my mimic* comes. When they him spy,   buffoon
As wild geese that the creeping fowler eye,

20

Or russet-pated choughs,* many in sort,*   crows/
                                                            i.e., together
Rising and cawing at the gun's report,
Sever themselves and madly sweep the sky,
So, at his sight, away his fellows fly;
And, at our stamp, here o'er and o'er one falls;
He murder cries and help from Athens calls.
Their sense thus weak, lost with their fears thus
    strong,
Made senseless things begin to do them wrong;
For briers and thorns at their apparel snatch;
Some sleeves, some hats, from yielders all things
    catch.   30
I led them on in this distracted fear,
And left sweet Pyramus translated there:
When in that moment, so it came to pass,
Titania waked and straightway loved an ass.

OBERON.

This falls out better than I could devise.
But hast thou yet latched* the Athenian's eyes   anointed
With the love-juice, as I did bid thee do?

PUCK.

I took him sleeping—that is finished too—
And the Athenian woman by his side;
That, when he waked, of force* she must be eyed.   necessity/40

(HERMIA *enters, followed by* DEMETRIUS.)

OBERON (*aside, to* PUCK, *as they move apart*).

Stand close:* this is the same Athenian.   concealed

PUCK (*aside, to* OBERON).

This is the woman, but not this the man.

DEMETRIUS (*to* HERMIA).

O, why rebuke you him that loves you so?
Lay breath so bitter on your bitter foe.

HERMIA (*to* DEMETRIUS).

Now I but chide; but I should use thee worse,
For thou, I fear, hast given me cause to curse.
If thou hast slain Lysander in his sleep,
Being o'er shoes in blood, plunge in the deep,
And kill me too.
The sun was not so true unto the day   **50**
As he to me. Would he have stolen away
From sleeping Hermia? I'll believe as soon
This whole earth may be bored and that the moon
May through the center creep and so displease
Her brother's noontide with the Antipodes.
It cannot be but thou hast murdered him;
So should a murderer look, so dead,* so grim.   deadly

DEMETRIUS.

So should the murdered look, and so should I,
Pierced through the heart with your stern cruelty.
Yet you, the murderer, look as bright, as clear,   **60**
As yonder Venus in her glimmering sphere.

HERMIA.

What's this to my Lysander? Where is he?
Ah, good Demetrius, wilt thou give him me?

DEMETRIUS.

I had rather give his carcass to my hounds.

HERMIA.

Out, dog! Out, cur! Thou drivest me past the
  bounds
Of maiden's patience. Hast thou slain him, then?
Henceforth be never numbered among men!
O, once tell true, tell true, even for my sake!
Durst thou have looked upon him being awake,
And hast thou killed him sleeping? O
  brave touch!*   noble deed/70
Could not a worm, an adder, do so much?
An adder did it; for with doubler tongue
Than thine, thou serpent, never adder stung.

DEMETRIUS.

You spend your passion on a misprised* mood:*   mistaken/
                                                      anger
I am not guilty of Lysander's blood;
Nor is he dead, for aught that I can tell.

HERMIA.

I pray thee, tell me then that he is well.

DEMETRIUS.

An if I could, what should I get therefor?

HERMIA.

A privilege never to see me more.
And from thy hated presence part I so.   80
See me no more, whether he be dead or no.
    (HERMIA *leaves*.)

DEMETRIUS.

There is no following her in this fierce vein.*   mood
Here therefore for a while I will remain.
So sorrow's heaviness doth heavier grow
For debt that bankrupt sleep doth sorrow owe;
Which now in some slight measure it will pay,
If for his tender* here I make some stay.   its offer
    (DEMETRIUS *lies down and sleeps.*)

OBERON (*to* PUCK).

What hast thou done? Thou hast mistaken quite
And laid the love-juice on some true-love's sight:
Of thy misprision must perforce ensue   90
Some true love turned and not a false turned true.

PUCK.

Then fate o'errules, that, one man holding troth,
A million fail, confounding oath on oath.

OBERON.

About the wood go swifter than the wind,
And Helena of Athens look thou find.
All fancy*-sick she is and pale of cheer,*   love/face
With sighs of love, that costs the fresh blood
    dear.³⁴
By some illusion see thou bring her here:
I'll charm his eyes against* she do appear.   before

PUCK.

                                  100
I go, I go; look how I go,
Swifter than arrow from the Tartar's bow.³⁵

(PUCK *goes.*)

OBERON (*squeezing juice of the flower into* DEME-
TRIUS' *eyes*).

> Flower of this purple dye,
> Hit with Cupid's archery,
> Sink in apple of his eye.
> When his love he doth espy,
> Let her shine as gloriously
> As the Venus of the sky.
> When thou wakest, if she be by,
> Beg of her for remedy.

(PUCK *returns.*)

PUCK.

> Captain of our fairy band,   110
> Helena is here at hand;
> And the youth, mistook by me,
> Pleading for a lover's fee.
> Shall we their fond* pageant see?   **foolish**
> Lord, what fools these mortals be!

OBERON.

> Stand aside: the noise they make
> Will cause Demetrius to awake.

PUCK.

> Then will two at once woo one;
> That must needs be sport alone;
> And those things do best please me   120
> That befall preposterously.

(*As* PUCK *and* OBERON *step aside,* HELENA *enters, followed by* LYSANDER.)

LYSANDER.

Why should you think that I should woo in scorn?
Scorn and derision never come in tears.
Look, when I vow, I weep; and vows so born,
In their nativity all truth appears.
How can these things in me seem scorn to you,
Bearing the badge of faith, to prove them true?

HELENA.

You do advance your cunning more and more.
   When truth kills truth, O devilish-holy fray!
These vows are Hermia's: will you give her o'er?*   up/130
   Weigh oath with oath, and you will nothing
     weigh.
Your vows to her and me, put in two scales,
Will even weigh, and both as light as tales.

LYSANDER.

I had no judgment when to her I swore.

HELENA.

Nor none, in my mind, now you give her o'er.

LYSANDER.

Demetrius loves her, and he loves not you.

DEMETRIUS (*awakening*).

O Helen, goddess, nymph, perfect, divine!
To what, my love, shall I compare thine eyne?
Crystal is muddy. O, how ripe in show

Thy lips, those kissing cherries, tempting grow!   140
That pure congealèd white, high Taurus' snow,[36]
Fanned with the eastern wind, turns to a crow
When thou hold'st up thy hand. O, let me kiss
This princess of pure white, this seal of bliss!
    (*Attempts to kiss her.*)

HELENA (*evading him, to both of them*).
O spite! O hell! I see you all are bent
To set against me for your merriment.
If you were civil and knew courtesy,
You would not do me thus much injury.
Can you not hate me, as I know you do,
But you must join in souls to mock me too?   150
If you were men, as men you are in show,
You would not use a gentle lady so;
To vow, and swear, and superpraise my parts,
When I am sure you hate me with all your hearts.
You both are rivals, and love Hermia;
And now both rivals, to mock Helena.
A trim* exploit, a manly enterprise,   fine
To conjure tears up in a poor maid's eyes
With your derision! None of noble sort
Would so offend a virgin and extort*   torture
A poor soul's patience, all to make you sport.   161

LYSANDER.
You are unkind, Demetrius; be not so;
For you love Hermia; this you know I know:
And here, with all good will, with all my heart,

In Hermia's love I yield you up my part;
And yours of Helena to me bequeath,
Whom I do love and will do till my death.

HELENA.

Never did mockers waste more idle breath.

DEMETRIUS.

Lysander, keep thy Hermia; I will none:*   *i.e.,* none
                                                        of her
                                                          170
If e'er I loved her, all that love is gone.
My heart to her but as guest-wise* sojourned,   a guest
And now to Helen is it home returned,
There to remain.

LYSANDER.   Helen, it is not so.

DEMETRIUS (*to* LYSANDER).

Disparage not the faith thou dost not know,
Lest, to thy peril, thou aby* it dear.   pay for
    Look, where thy love comes: yonder is thy dear.
    (HERMIA *returns.*)

HERMIA (*to* LYSANDER).

Dark night, that from the eye his* function takes,   its
The ear more quick of apprehension makes;
Wherein it doth impair the seeing sense,
It pays the hearing double recompense.   180
Thou art not by mine eye, Lysander, found;
Mine ear, I thank it, brought me to thy sound.
But why unkindly didst thou leave me so?

LYSANDER.

Why should he stay, whom love doth press to go?

HERMIA.

What love could press Lysander from my side?

LYSANDER.

Lysander's love, that would not let him bide,
Fair Helena, who more engilds the night
Than all yon fiery oes* and eyes of light.   circles
Why seek'st thou me? Could not this make thee
 know,
The hate I bear thee made me leave thee so?   190

HERMIA.

You speak not as you think: it cannot be.

HELENA.

Lo, she is one of this confederacy!
Now I perceive they have conjoined all three
To fashion this false sport, in spite of me.
 Injurious* Hermia! Most ungrateful maid!   insulting
Have you conspired, have you with these
 contrived
To bait me with this foul derision?
Is all the counsel that we two have shared,
The sisters' vows, the hours that we have spent,
When we have chid the hasty-footed time   200
For parting us—O, is it all forgot?
All school-days' friendship, childhood innocence?
We, Hermia, like two artificial* gods,   skilled
              in art
Have with our needles created both one flower,
Both on one sampler, sitting on one cushion,
Both warbling of one song, both in one key,

As if our hands, our sides, voices and minds,
Had been incorporate.* So we grew together,   organic
Like to a double cherry, seeming parted,
But yet an union in partition: 210
Two lovely berries molded on one stem;
So, with two seeming bodies, but one heart;
Two of the first, like coats in heraldry,
Due but to one and crownèd with one crest.[37]
And will you rent our ancient love asunder,
To join with men in scorning your poor friend?
It is not friendly, 'tis not maidenly.
Our sex, as well as I, may chide you for it,
Though I alone do feel the injury.

HERMIA.

I am amazèd at your passionate words.   220
I scorn you not: it seems that you scorn me.

HELENA.

Have you not set Lysander, as in scorn,
To follow me and praise my eyes and face?
And made your other love, Demetrius,
Who even but now did spurn me with his foot,
To call me goddess, nymph, divine and rare,
Precious, celestial? Wherefore speaks he this
To her he hates? And wherefore doth Lysander
Deny your love, so rich within his soul,
And tender me, forsooth, affection,   230
But by your setting on, by your consent?

What though I be not so in grace as you,
So hung upon with love, so fortunate,
But miserable most, to love unloved?
This you should pity rather than despise.

HERMIA.

I understand not what you mean by this.

HELENA.

Ay, do, persever, counterfeit sad* looks,   grave
Make mouths upon me* when I turn my back;   faces at me
Wink each at other; hold the sweet jest up:
This sport, well carried, shall be chronicled.   240
If you have any pity, grace, or manners,
You would not make me* such an argument.   make me
                                                 subject for
    (*Starting to leave.*)
But fare ye well: 'tis partly my own fault;
Which death or absence soon shall remedy.

LYSANDER (*stopping her*).

Stay, gentle Helena; hear my excuse.
My love, my life, my soul, fair Helena!

HELENA.

O excellent!

HERMIA (*to* LYSANDER).

                Sweet, do not scorn her so.

DEMETRIUS (*to* LYSANDER).

If she cannot entreat, I can compel.

LYSANDER (*to* DEMETRIUS).

Thou canst compel no more than she entreat:

Thy threats have no more strength than her weak
    prayers.   **250**

Helen, I love thee; by my life, I do:

I swear by that which I will lose for thee,

To prove him false that says I love thee not.

DEMETRIUS (*to* HELENA).

I say I love thee more than he can do.

LYSANDER (*to* DEMETRIUS).

If thou say so, withdraw, and prove it too.

DEMETRIUS.

Quick, come!

HERMIA.   Lysander, whereto tends all this?

LYSANDER (*to* HERMIA, *as she tries to restrain him*).

Away, you Ethiope!

DEMETRIUS (*to* HERMIA).

        No, no; he'll . . .

    (*To* LYSANDER.)

Seem to break loose; take on as you would follow,

But yet come not. You are a tame man, go!

LYSANDER (*to* HERMIA, *who still clings to him*).

Hang off,* thou cat, thou burr! Vile thing,   let go
    let loose,   **260**

Or I will shake thee from me like a serpent!

HERMIA.

Why are you grown so rude? What change is
    this?

Sweet love—

LYSANDER.   Thy love! Out, tawny Tartar, out!
Out, loathèd medicine! Hated potion, hence!

HERMIA.
Do you not jest?

HELENA.   Yes, sooth; and so do you.

LYSANDER (*to* DEMETRIUS, *while still struggling to free
   himself*).
Demetrius, I will keep my word with thee.

DEMETRIUS.
I would I had your bond, for I perceive.
A weak bond holds you. I'll not trust your word.

LYSANDER.
What, should I hurt her, strike her, kill her dead?
Although I hate her, I'll not harm her so.   **270**

HERMIA.
What, can you do me greater harm than hate?
Hate me! Wherefore? O me! What news,*   what's
   my love!   happened
Am not I Hermia? Are not you Lysander?
I am as fair now as I was erewhile.
Since night you loved me; yet since night you
   left me.
Why, then you left me—O, the gods forbid!—
In earnest, shall I say?

LYSANDER.   Ay, by my life;
And never did desire to see thee more.
Therefore be out of hope, of question, of doubt.

Be certain, nothing truer: 'tis no jest   **280**
That I do hate thee and love Helena.

HERMIA (*to* HELENA, *releasing* LYSANDER).

O me! You juggler! You canker*-blossom!   **wormy**
You thief of love! What, have you come by **night**
And stolen my love's heart from him?

HELENA (*to* HERMIA).   Fine, i' faith!

Have you no modesty, no maiden shame,
No touch of bashfulness? What, will you tear
Impatient answers from my gentle tongue?
Fie, fie! You counterfeit, you puppet, you!

HERMIA.

Puppet? Why so? Ay, that way goes the game.
Now I perceive that she hath made compare   **290**
Between our statures; she hath urged her height;
And with her personage, her tall personage,
Her height, forsooth, she hath prevailed with him.
And are you grown so high in his esteem,
Because I am so dwarfish and so low?
How low am I, thou painted maypole? Speak;
How low am I? I am not yet so low
But that my nails can reach unto thine eyes.

        (*Starts to attack* HELENA.)

HELENA.

I pray you, though you mock me, gentlemen,
Let her not hurt me. I was never curst;*   **shrewish**
I have no gift at all in shrewishness;   **301**

I am a right* maid for my cowardice: typical
Let her not strike me. You perhaps may think,
Because she is something lower than myself,
That I can match her.

HERMIA.   Lower! Hark, again.

    (*Threatens* HELENA.)

HELENA.

Good Hermia, do not be so bitter with me.
I evermore did love you, Hermia,
Did ever keep your counsels, never wronged you,
Save that, in love unto Demetrius,
I told him of your stealth* into this wood.   *i.e.,* stealthy
                                            flight
He followed you; for love I followed him;   311
But he hath chid me hence and threatened me
To strike me, spurn me, nay, to kill me too.
And now, so you will let me quiet go,
To Athens will I bear my folly back
And follow you no further. Let me go.
You see how simple and how fond* I am.   foolish

HERMIA.

Why, get you gone. Who is 't that hinders you?

HELENA.

A foolish heart, that I leave here behind.

HERMIA.

What, with Lysander?

HELENA.   With Demetrius.   320

    (HERMIA *threatens* HELENA *again.*)

LYSANDER.

Be not afraid; she shall not harm thee, Helena.

DEMETRIUS.

No, sir, she shall not, though you take her part.

HELENA.

O, when she's angry, she is keen and shrewd!*   sharp-tongued
She was a vixen when she went to school;
And though she be but little, she is fierce.

HERMIA.

"Little" again! nothing but "low" and "little"!
Why will you suffer her to flout me thus?
Let me come to her.

LYSANDER.   Get you gone, you dwarf;
You minimus,* of hindering knot-grass made;[38]   minimum
You bead, you acorn.

DEMETRIUS (*to* LYSANDER).

                    You are too officious   330
In her behalf that scorns your services.
Let her alone. Speak not of Helena;
Take not her part; for, if thou dost intend*   extend
Never so little show of love to her,
Thou shalt aby* it.   pay for

LYSANDER (*to* DEMETRIUS).

                    Now she holds me not;
Now follow, if thou darest, to try whose right,
Of thine or mine, is most in Helena.

DEMETRIUS.

Follow! Nay, I'll go with thee, cheek by jole.*   jowl

(LYSANDER *and* DEMETRIUS *go off.*)

HERMIA (*to* HELENA).

You, mistress, all this coil* is 'long* of you.   turmoil/
    (*As* HELENA *retreats.*)   because
Nay, go not back.

HELENA.   I will not trust you, I,   340
Nor longer stay in your curst company.
Your hands than mine are quicker for a fray,
My legs are longer though, to run away.
    (HELENA *runs out.*)

HERMIA.

I am amazed, and know not what to say.
    (HERMIA *leaves.*)

OBERON (*to* PUCK).

This is thy negligence: still* thou mistakest,   always
Or else committ'st thy knaveries willfully.

PUCK.

Believe me, king of shadows, I mistook.
Did not you tell me I should know the man
By the Athenian garments he had on?
And so far blameless proves my enterprise,   350
That I have 'nointed an Athenian's eyes;
And so far am I glad it so did sort*   turn out
As this their jangling I esteem a sport.

OBERON.

Thou see'st these lovers seek a place to fight.
Hie therefore, Robin, overcast the night.
The starry welkin cover thou anon

With drooping fog as black as Acheron,[39]
And lead these testy rivals so astray
As one come not within another's way.
Like to Lysander sometime frame thy tongue,   360
Then stir Demetrius up with bitter wrong;*   *i.e.,* insults
And sometime rail thou like Demetrius;
And from each other look thou lead them thus,
Till o'er their brows death-counterfeiting sleep
With leaden legs and batty wings doth creep:
    (*Giving him a herb.*)
Then crush this herb into Lysander's eye;
Whose liquor hath this virtuous* property,   potent
To take from thence all error with his might,*   its power
And make his eyeballs roll with wonted sight.
When they next wake, all this derision   370
Shall seem a dream and fruitless vision,
And back to Athens shall the lovers wend,
With league* whose date till death shall never end.   union
Whiles I in this affair do thee employ,
I'll to my queen and beg her Indian boy:
And then I will her charmèd eye release
From monster's view, and all things shall be peace.

PUCK.

My fairy lord, this must be done with haste,
For night's swift dragons cut the clouds full fast,[40]
And yonder shines Aurora's harbinger;[41]   380
At whose approach, ghosts, wandering here and
    there,

Troop home to churchyards; damned spirits all,
That in crossways and floods have burial,[42]
Already to their wormy beds are gone.
For fear lest day should look their shames upon,
They willfully themselves exile from light
And must for aye consort with black-browed
  night.

OBERON.

But we are spirits of another sort:[43]
I with the morning's love have oft made sport,[44]
And, like a forester, the groves may tread,   390
Even till the eastern gate, all fiery-red,
Opening on Neptune with fair blessèd beams,[45]
Turns into yellow gold his salt green streams.
But—notwithstanding—haste; make no delay:
We may effect this business yet ere day.
   (OBERON *goes.*)

PUCK (*chanting, as he casts his spell*).

   Up and down, up and down,
   I will lead them up and down.
   I am feared in field and town:
   Goblin, lead them up and down.

Here comes one.   400
   (LYSANDER *enters, feeling his way as if in a fog.*)

LYSANDER.

Where art thou, proud Demetrius? Speak thou
  now.

PUCK (*imitating* DEMETRIUS' *voice*).
Here, villain; drawn and ready. Where art thou?
LYSANDER (*moving toward voice*).
I will be with thee straight.
PUCK (*in* DEMETRIUS' *voice, as he moves off*).
                           Follow me, then,
To plainer* ground.   **more level**
    (*As* LYSANDER *leaves, following* PUCK's *voice,* DE-
    METRIUS *enters, feeling his way.*)
DEMETRIUS.   Lysander! Speak again:
Thou runaway, thou coward, art thou fled?
Speak! In some bush? Where dost thou hide thy
    head?
PUCK (*returning, and imitating* LYSANDER's *voice*).
Thou coward, art thou bragging to the stars,
Telling the bushes that thou look'st for wars,
And wilt not come? Come, recreant; come, thou
    child,
I'll whip thee with a rod. He is defiled   **410**
That draws a sword on thee.
DEMETRIUS   Yea, art thou there?
PUCK (*in* LYSANDER's *voice, as he moves off*).
Follow my voice: we'll try no manhood here.
    (*As* DEMETRIUS *leaves, following* PUCK's *voice,*
    LYSANDER *re-enters.*)
LYSANDER.
He goes before me and still dares me on.
When I come where he calls, then he is gone.

The villain is much lighter-heeled than I:
I followed fast, but faster he did fly;
That fallen am I in dark uneven way,
And here will rest me.

    (*Lies down.*)   Come, thou gentle day!
For if but once thou show me thy gray light,
I'll find Demetrius and revenge this spite.   **420**

    (*He falls asleep.* PUCK *re-enters, followed by* DE-
METRIUS.)

PUCK (*in* LYSANDER's *voice*).

Ho, ho, ho! Coward, why comest thou not?

DEMETRIUS.

Abide me, if thou darest; for well I wot*   **know**
Thou runn'st before me, shifting every place,
And darest not stand, nor look me in the face.
Where art thou now?

PUCK (*from another spot, in* LYSANDER's *voice*).

                Come hither: I am here.

DEMETRIUS.

Nay, then, thou mock'st me. Thou shalt buy
    this dear,
If ever I thy face by daylight see.
Now, go thy way. Faintness constraineth me
To measure out my length on this cold bed.
By day's approach look to be visited.   **430**

    (DEMETRIUS *lies down and falls asleep.* HELENA
enters, as if lost in a fog.)

HELENA.

O weary night, O long and tedious night,
  Abate thy hours! Shine comforts from the east,
That I may back to Athens by daylight,
  From these that my poor company detest:
And sleep, that sometimes shuts up sorrow's eye,
Steal me awhile from mine own company.
  (*Lies down and falls asleep.*)

PUCK.

  Yet but three? Come one more;
  Two of both kinds makes up four.
  Here she comes, curst* and sad: shrewish
  Cupid is a knavish lad,   440
  Thus to make poor females mad.
  (HERMIA *enters, as if lost in a fog.*)

HERMIA.

Never so weary, never so in woe,
  Bedabbled with the dew and torn with briers,
I can no further crawl, no further go;
  My legs can keep no pace with my desires.
Here will I rest me till the break of day.
Heavens shield Lysander, if they mean a fray!
  (*Lies down and falls asleep.*)

PUCK.

  On the ground
  Sleep sound:
  I'll apply   450
  To your eye,

Gentle lover, remedy.
(*Squeezes juice of the herb on* LYSANDER's *eyes.*)
When thou wakest,
Thou takest
True delight
In the sight
Of thy former lady's eye.
And the country proverb known,
That every man should take his own,
In your waking shall be shown: **460**
Jack shall have Jill;
Nought shall go ill;
The man shall have his mare again,[46] and all shall
be well.
(PUCK *goes.*)

ACT IV

Scene 1. The same portion of the wood.

(LYSANDER, DEMETRIUS, HELENA, *and* HERMIA *are still asleep.* TITANIA *and* BOTTOM *enter, attended by* PEASEBLOSSOM, COBWEB, MOTH, MUSTARDSEED, *and other* FAIRIES, *with* OBERON *watching from behind.*)

TITANIA.
  Come, sit thee down upon this flowery bed,
    While I thy amiable cheeks do coy,*   stroke
  And stick musk-roses in thy sleek smooth head,
    And kiss thy fair large ears, my gentle joy.
BOTTOM (*sitting*).
  Where's Peaseblossom?
PEASEBLOSSOM (*coming forward*).
  Ready.
BOTTOM.
  Scratch my head, Peaseblossom. (*As* PEASEBLOSSOM
  does so.) Where's Mounsieur Cobweb?
COBWEB (*coming forward*).
  Ready.

107

BOTTOM.

Mounsieur Cobweb, good mounsieur, get you   10
your weapons in your hand, and kill me a red-
hipped humble-bee on the top of a thistle; and
good mounsieur, bring me the honey-bag. Do not
fret yourself too much in the action, mounsieur;
and, good mounsieur, have a care the honey-bag
break not; I would be loath to have you overflown
with a honey-bag, signior. (COBWEB *goes.*) Where's
Mounsieur Mustardseed?

MUSTARDSEED (*coming forward*).
Ready.

BOTTOM.

Give me your neaf,* Mounsieur Mustardseed.   fist/20
Pray you, leave your courtesy,* good mounsieur.   *i.e.,* never
                                                      mind

MUSTARDSEED.
What's your will?

BOTTOM.

Nothing, good mounsieur, but to help Cavalery*   *i.e.,*
Cobweb to scratch. (MUSTARDSEED *scratches him.*)   gentleman
I must to the barber's, mounsieur; for methinks I
am marvelous hairy about the face; and I am such
a tender ass, if my hair do but tickle me, I must
scratch.

TITANIA.
What, wilt thou hear some music, my sweet love?

BOTTOM.

I have a reasonable good ear in music. Let's have   30

the tongs and the bones.*

TITANIA.

Or say, sweet love, what thou desirest to eat.

BOTTOM.

Truly, a peck of provender. I could munch your
good dry oats. Methinks I have a great desire to
a bottle* of hay: good hay, sweet hay, hath no
fellow.

TITANIA.

I have a venturous fairy that shall seek
The squirrel's hoard, and fetch thee new nuts.

BOTTOM.

I had rather have a handful or two of dried peas.
But, I pray you, let none of your people stir me:
I have an exposition of* sleep come upon me.

TITANIA.

Sleep thou, and I will wind thee in my arms.
Fairies, be gone, and be all ways away.

    (*The* FAIRIES *leave, and* TITANIA *cradles* BOTTOM
in her arms.)

So doth the woodbine the sweet honeysuckle
Gentle entwist; the female ivy so
Enrings the barky fingers of the elm.
O, how I love thee! How I dote on thee!

    (TITANIA *and* BOTTOM *fall asleep.* PUCK *enters,
and* OBERON *brings him forward so they both*

Margin glosses:

triangle
and
clappers

bundle

40

disposi-
tion to

look down on the sleeping TITANIA *and* BOTTOM.)

OBERON.

Welcome, good Robin. See'st thou this sweet
    sight?
Her dotage now I do begin to pity;   50
For, meeting her of late behind the wood,
Seeking sweet favors for this hateful fool,
I did upbraid her and fall out with her;
For she his hairy temples then had rounded
With coronet of fresh and fragrant flowers;
And that same dew, which sometime on the buds
Was wont to swell like round and orient* pearls,   lustrous
Stood now within the pretty flowerets' eyes
Like tears that did their own disgrace bewail.
When I had at my pleasure taunted her   60
And she in mild terms begged my patience,
I then did ask of her her changeling child;
Which straight she gave me, and her fairy sent
To bear him to my bower in fairy land.
And now I have the boy, I will undo
This hateful imperfection of her eyes.
And, gentle Puck, take this transformed scalp
From off the head of this Athenian swain,
That, he awaking when the other* do,   others
May all to Athens back again repair   70
And think no more of this night's accidents
But as the fierce vexation of a dream.

But first I will release the fairy queen.
(*Squeezing juice from a flower into* TITANIA'*s eyes.*)

> Be as thou wast wont to be;
> See as thou wast wont to see.
>> Dian's bud o'er Cupid's flower[47]
>> Hath such force and blessèd power.

Now, my Titania: wake you, my sweet queen.

TITANIA (*waking*).

My Oberon! What visions have I seen!
Methought I was enamored of an ass.   80

OBERON.

There lies your love.

TITANIA (*discovering the sleeping* BOTTOM.)
                How came these things to pass?
O, how mine eyes do loathe his visage now!

OBERON.

Silence awhile. Robin, take off this head.
Titania, music call; and strike more dead*   *i.e.,* deep
Than common* sleep of all these five the sense.*   normal/
                                                       senses

TITANIA.

Music, ho! Music, such as charmeth sleep!
(*Music is heard.*)

PUCK (*removing the ass's head*).

Now, when thou wakest, with thine own fool's
  eyes peep.

OBERON.

Sound, music! Come, my queen, take hands

with me,
And rock the ground whereon these sleepers be.   90
Now thou and I are new in amity
And will tomorrow midnight solemnly
Dance in Duke Theseus' house triumphantly
And bless it to all fair prosperity.
There shall the pairs of faithful lovers be
Wedded, with Theseus, all in jollity.

PUCK.

Fairy king, attend, and mark:
I do hear the morning lark.

OBERON.

Then, my queen, in silence sad,*   serious
Trip we after night's shade: 100
We the globe can compass soon,
Swifter than the wandering moon.

TITANIA.

Come, my lord, and in our flight
Tell me how it came this night
That I sleeping here was found
With these mortals on the ground.

(OBERON, TITANIA, *and* PUCK *go. After a moment,*
horns sound, and a hunting party enters, led by
THESEUS, HIPPOLYTA, *and* EGEUS.)

THESEUS (*to an* ATTENDANT).

Go, one of you, find out the forester;
For now our observation* is performed;   observance

And since we have the vaward* of the day,   vanguard
My love shall hear the music of my hounds.[48]   110
Uncouple in the western valley; let them go:
Dispatch,* I say, and find the forester.   hurry
 (*The* ATTENDANT *goes.*)
We will, fair queen, up to the mountain's top
And mark the musical confusion
Of hounds and echo in conjunction.

HIPPOLYTA.

I was with Hercules and Cadmus once,[49]
When in a wood of Crete they bayed the bear
With hounds of Sparta: never did I hear
Such gallant chiding;* for, besides the groves,   clamor
The skies, the fountains, every region near   120
Seemed all one mutual cry. I never heard
So musical a discord, such sweet thunder.

THESEUS.

My hounds are bred out of the Spartan kind,
So flewed,* so sanded,* and their heads are hung eared/
               sandy-colored
With ears that sweep away the morning dew;
Crook-kneed, and dew-lapped like Thessalian bulls;
Slow in pursuit, but matched in mouth like bells,
Each under each. A cry* more tunable   pack
Was never holla'd to, nor cheered with horn,
In Crete, in Sparta, nor in Thessaly.   130
Judge when you hear.
 (*Seeing the sleepers.*)
     But, soft! What nymphs are these?

EGEUS.

My lord, this is my daughter here asleep;
And this, Lysander; this Demetrius is;
This Helena, old Nedar's Helena:
I wonder of their being here together.

THESEUS.

No doubt they rose up early to observe
The rite of May, and, hearing our intent,
Came here in grace of our solemnity.*   ceremony
But speak, Egeus; is not this the day
That Hermia should give answer of her choice? **140**

EGEUS.

It is, my lord.

THESEUS (*to an* ATTENDANT).

Go, bid the huntsmen wake them with their horns.
 (ATTENDANT *goes. Horns sound, and shouting is*
 heard. LYSANDER, DEMETRIUS, HELENA, *and* HERMIA
 wake up.)
Good morrow, friends. Saint Valentine is past:
Begin these wood-birds but to couple now?[50]

LYSANDER.

Pardon, my lord.

THESEUS.   I pray you all, stand up.
 (*The couples rise. To* LYSANDER *and* DEMETRIUS.)
I know you two are rival enemies:
How comes this gentle concord in the world,
That hatred is so far from jealousy,
To sleep by hate, and fear no enmity?

LYSANDER.

My lord, I shall reply amazedly,   150
Half sleep, half waking: but as yet, I swear,
I cannot truly say how I came here;
But, as I think—for truly would I speak
And now I do bethink me, so it is—
I came with Hermia hither. Our intent
Was to be gone from Athens, where* we might,   wherever
Without* the peril of the Athenian law.   outside of

EGEUS.

Enough, enough, my lord; you have enough.
I beg the law, the law, upon his head.
They would have stolen away; they would,
    Demetrius,   160
Thereby to have defeated you and me,
You of your wife and me of my consent,
Of my consent that she should be your wife.

DEMETRIUS.

My lord, fair Helen told me of their stealth,
Of this their purpose hither to this wood;
And I in fury* hither followed them,   out of love
Fair Helena in fancy following me.
But, my good lord, I wot not by what power—
But by some power it is—my love to Hermia,
Melted as the snow, seems to me now   170
As the remembrance of an idle gawd*   worthless
                                                              trifle
Which in my childhood I did dote upon;
And all the faith, the virtue of my heart,

The object and the pleasure of mine eye,
Is only Helena. To her, my lord,
Was I betrothed ere I saw Hermia;
But, like in sickness, did I loathe this food.
But, as in health, come to my natural taste,
Now I do wish it, love it, long for it,
And will for evermore be true to it.   180

THESEUS.

Fair lovers, you are fortunately met.
Of this discourse we more will hear anon.
Egeus, I will overbear your will;
For in the temple, by and by,* with us   at once
These couples shall eternally be knit;
And, for the morning now is something worn,
Our purposed hunting shall be set aside.
    Away with us to Athens; three and three,
We'll hold a feast in great solemnity.
Come, Hippolyta.   190

    (THESEUS *leads* HIPPOLYTA *away, followed by*
    EGEUS *and his train.*)

DEMETRIUS.

These things seem small and undistinguishable,
Like far-off mountains turnèd into clouds.

HERMIA.

Methinks I see these things with parted* eye   *i.e.,*
When everything seems double.   unfocused

HELENA.   So methinks.

And I have found Demetrius like a jewel,

Mine own, and not mine own.

DEMETRIUS.   Are you sure
That we are awake? It seems to me
That yet we sleep, we dream. Do not you think
The duke was here, and bid us follow him?

HERMIA.

Yea; and my father.

HELENA.   And Hippolyta.   **200**

LYSANDER.

And he did bid us follow to the temple.

DEMETRIUS.

Why, then, we are awake. Let 's follow him,
And by the way let us recount our dreams.

> (LYSANDER, DEMETRIUS, HELENA, *and* HERMIA *leave.*
> *After a moment,* BOTTOM, *till now concealed in
> the bower, awakes.*)

BOTTOM.

When my cue comes, call me, and I will answer:
my next is, "Most fair Pyramus." Heigh-ho!

Peter Quince! Flute, the bellows-mender! Snout,
the tinker! Starveling!

God's my life, stolen hence, and left me asleep!
I have had a most rare vision. I have had a dream,
past the wit of man to say what dream it was: man   **210**
is but an ass, if he go about* to expound this   attempt
dream. Methought I was—there is no man can tell
what. Methought I was—and methought I had—

but man is but a patched* fool, if he will offer to   motley
say what methought I had. The eye of man hath
not heard, the ear of man hath not seen, man's
hand is not able to taste, his tongue to conceive,
nor his heart to report, what my dream was. I will
get Peter Quince to write a ballad of this dream: 220
it shall be called Bottom's Dream, because it hath
no bottom; and I will sing it in the latter end of
a play, before the duke. Peradventure, to make it
the more gracious, I shall sing it at her* death.   *i.e.,*
(BOTTOM *leaves.*)   Thisbe's

SCENE 2. Athens. A room in QUINCE's house.

(QUINCE, FLUTE, SNOUT, *and* STARVELING *enter.*)

QUINCE.

Have you sent to Bottom's house? Is he come
home yet?

STARVELING.

He cannot be heard of. Out of doubt he is transported.

FLUTE.

If he come not, then the play is marred. It goes
not forward, doth it?

QUINCE.

It is not possible: you have not a man in all Athens
able to discharge Pyramus but he.

FLUTE.

No, he hath simply the best wit of any handicraft man in Athens.   10

QUINCE.

Yea, and the best person too; and he is a very paramour for a sweet voice.

FLUTE.

You must say "paragon": a paramour is, God bless us, a thing of naught.*   wicked
thing

(SNUG *enters.*)

SNUG.

Masters, the duke is coming from the temple, and there is two or three lords and ladies more married. If our sport had gone forward, we had all been made men.

FLUTE.

O sweet bully Bottom! Thus hath he lost sixpence a day during his life; he could not have 'scaped   20
sixpence a day: an the duke had not given him sixpence a day for playing Pyramus, I'll be hanged. He would have deserved it. Sixpence a day in Pyramus, or nothing.

(BOTTOM *enters.*)

BOTTOM.

Where are these lads? Where are these hearts?*   good
fellows

QUINCE.

Bottom! O most courageous day! O most happy hour!

BOTTOM.

Masters, I am to discourse wonders, but ask me
not what; for if I tell you, I am no true Athenian.   30
I will tell you everything, right as it fell out.

QUINCE.

Let us hear, sweet Bottom.

BOTTOM.

Not a word of me. All that I will tell you is, that
the duke hath dined. Get your apparel together,
good strings to your beards, new ribbons to your
pumps; meet presently* at the palace; every man   at once
look o'er his part; for the short and the long is,
our play is preferred. In any case, let Thisby have   40
clean linen; and let not him that plays the lion pare
his nails, for they shall hang out for the lion's
claws. And, most dear actors, eat no onions nor
garlic, for we are to utter sweet breath; and I do
not doubt but to hear them say, it is a sweet
comedy. No more words. Away! Go! Away!

(*They go.*)

ACT V

SCENE 1. Athens. The great hall in the palace of THESEUS.

(THESEUS *and* HIPPOLYTA *enter, followed by* PHILOSTRATE, LORDS *and* ATTENDANTS.)

HIPPOLYTA.
    'Tis strange, my Theseus, that* these lovers   *that which*
      speak of.

THESEUS.
    More strange than true. I never may believe
    These antique fables, nor these fairy toys.*   *trifles*
    Lovers and madmen have such seething brains,
    Such shaping fantasies, that apprehend
    More than cool reason ever comprehends.
    The lunatic, the lover, and the poet
    Are of imagination all compact.[51]
    One sees more devils than vast hell can hold:
    That is, the madman. The lover, all as frantic,   10
    Sees Helen's beauty in a brow of Egypt.[52]
    The poet's eye, in a fine frenzy rolling,
    Doth glance from heaven to earth, from earth to
      heaven;

51, 52, See Notes, p. 215.

And as imagination bodies forth
The forms of things unknown, the poet's pen
Turns them to shapes and gives to airy nothing
A local habitation and a name.
Such tricks hath strong imagination
That, if it would but apprehend some joy,
It comprehends* some bringer of that joy;[53]   includes
Or in the night, imagining some fear,   21
How easy is a bush supposed a bear!

HIPPOLYTA.

But all the story of the night told over,
And all their minds transfigured so together,
More witnesseth* than fancy's images   testifies
And grows to something of great constancy;*   to more
But, howsoever, strange. and admirable.   certainty

THESEUS.

Here come the lovers, full of joy and mirth.

(LYSANDER, DEMETRIUS, HERMIA, *and* HELENA *enter.*)

Joy, gentle friends! Joy and fresh days of love
Accompany your hearts!

LYSANDER.   More than to us   30
Wait in your royal walks, your board, your bed!

THESEUS.

Come now; what masques, what dances shall we
    have,
To wear away this long age of three hours
Between our after-supper and bedtime?

Where is our usual manager of mirth?
What revels are in hand? Is there no play,
To ease the anguish of a torturing hour?
Call Philostrate.

PHILOSTRATE (*stepping forward*).
               Here, mighty Theseus.

THESEUS.
Say, what abridgment* have you for this evening?   *pastime*
What masque? What music? How shall we
  beguile   40
The lazy time, if not with some delight?

PHILOSTRATE.
There is a brief* how many sports are ripe: *list*
Make choice of which your highness will see first.
    (*Gives* THESEUS *a list.*)

THESEUS (*reads*).
"The battle with the Centaurs,[54] to be sung
By an Athenian eunuch to the harp."
We'll none of that: that have I told my love,
In glory of my kinsman Hercules.
    (*Reads.*)
"The riot of the tipsy Bacchanals,
Tearing the Thracian singer* in their rage."[55]   *i.e.,*
That is an old device; and it was played   *Orpheus*
When I from Thebes came last a conqueror.   50
    (*Reads.*)
"The thrice three Muses mourning for the death

Of Learning, late deceased in beggary."⁵⁶
That is some satire, keen and critical,
Not sorting* with a nuptial ceremony.   **in harmony**
    (*Reads.*)
"A tedious brief scene of young Pyramus
And his love Thisbe; very tragical mirth."
Merry and tragical! Tedious and brief!
    That is, hot ice and wondrous strange snow.
How shall we find the concord of this discord?   **60**

PHILOSTRATE.

A play there is, my lord, some ten words long,
Which is as brief as I have known a play;
But by ten words, my lord, it is too long,
Which makes it tedious; for in all the play
There is not one word apt, one player fitted.
And tragical, my noble lord, it is;
For Pyramus therein doth kill himself.
Which, when I saw rehearsed, I must confess,
Made mine eyes water; but more merry tears
The passion of loud laughter never shed.   **70**

THESEUS.

What are they that do play it?

PHILOSTRATE.

Hard-handed men that work in Athens here,
Which never labored in their minds till now
And now have toiled their unbreathed* memories   **untrained**
With this same play, against your nuptial.

THESEUS.

And we will hear it.

PHILOSTRATE.   No, my noble lord;

It is not for you. I have heard it over,

And it is nothing, nothing in the world;

Unless you can find sport in their intents,

Extremely stretched* and conned with cruel pain,   strained

To do you service.

THESEUS.   I will hear that play;   81

For never anything can be amiss,

When simpleness and duty tender it.

        (*As* PHILOSTRATE *exits, all take their seats.*)

Go, bring them in. And take your places, ladies.

HIPPOLYTA (*to* THESEUS).

I love not to see wretchedness o'ercharged*   overburdened

And duty in his* service perishing.   its

THESEUS.

Why, gentle sweet, you shall see no such thing.

HIPPOLYTA.

He says they can do nothing in this kind.

THESEUS.

The kinder we, to give them thanks for nothing.

Our sport* shall be to take what they mistake: entertainment
And what poor duty cannot do, noble respect   91

Takes it in might, not merit.[57]

Where* I have come, great clerks* have purposèd   whence/
scholars
To greet me with premeditated welcomes;

Where I have seen them shiver and look pale,
Make periods in the midst of sentences,
Throttle their practiced accent in their fears
And in conclusion dumbly have broke off,
Not paying me a welcome. Trust me, sweet,
Out of this silence yet I picked a welcome;   100
And in the modesty* of fearful duty   embarrass-
I read as much as from the rattling tongue   ment
Of saucy and audacious eloquence.
Love, therefore, and tongue-tied simplicity
In least speak most, to my capacity.*   compre-
    (PHILOSTRATE *returns*.)   hension

PHILOSTRATE.

So please your grace, the Prologue is addressed.*   ready

THESEUS.

Let him approach.

    (*Trumpets sound*. PETER QUINCE *steps forward
as the* PROLOGUE.)

PROLOGUE (QUINCE).

If we offend, it is with our good will.[58]
    That you should think, we come not to offend,
But with good will. To show our simple skill,   110
    That is the true beginning of our end.
Consider then we come but in despite.
    We do not come as minding to content you,
Our true intent is. All for your delight
    We are not here. That you should here repent

you.
The actors are at hand and by their show
You shall know all that you are like to know.

THESEUS.
This fellow doth not stand upon points.*   punctuation

LYSANDER.
He hath rid his prologue like a rough colt; he
knows not the stop.[59] A good moral, my lord: it
is not enough to speak, but to speak true.   120

HIPPOLYTA.
Indeed he hath played on his prologue like a child
on a recorder; a sound, but not in government.*   under
          control
THESEUS.
His speech was like a tangled chain; nothing im-
paired, but all disordered. Who is next?

 (BOTTOM *as* PYRAMUS, FLUTE *as* THISBE, SNOUT *as*
 WALL, STARVELING *as* MOONSHINE, *and* SNUG *as* LION
 now step forward.)

PROLOGUE (QUINCE).
Gentles,* perchance you wonder at this show;   *i.e.,* ladies
 and
But wonder on, till truth make all things plain. gentlemen
 (*Points out the characters, one by one.*)
This man is Pyramus, if you would know;   130
 This beauteous lady Thisby is certain.
This man, with lime and rough-cast, doth present
 Wall, that vile Wall which did these lovers
  sunder;

And through Wall's chink, poor souls, they are content
   To whisper. At the which let no man wonder.
This man, with lanthorn, dog, and bush of thorn,
   Presenteth Moonshine; for, if you will know,
By moonshine did these lovers think no scorn
   To meet at Ninus' tomb, there, there to woo.
This grisly beast, which Lion hight* by name.   is called
The trusty Thisby, coming first by night,   141
Did scare away, or rather did affright;
And, as she fled, her mantle she did fall,*   *i.e.,* let fall
   Which Lion vile with bloody mouth did stain.
Anon comes Pyramus, sweet youth and tall,*   brave
   And finds his trusty Thisby's mantle slain;
Whereat, with blade, with bloody blameful blade,
   He bravely broached* his boiling bloody breast; opened
And Thisby, tarrying in mulberry shade,
   His dagger drew, and died. For all the rest,   150
Let Lion, Moonshine, Wall, and lovers twain
At large discourse, while here they do remain.
   (PROLOGUE [QUINCE], PYRAMUS [BOTTOM], THISBE
   [FLUTE], LION [SNUG], *and* MOONSHINE [STARVE-
   LING] *leave.*)

THESEUS.

I wonder if the lion be* to speak.   is

DEMETRIUS.

No wonder, my lord. One lion may, when many
asses do.

WALL (SNOUT) (*stepping forward*).

In this same interlude it doth befall

That I, one Snout by name, present a wall;

And such a wall, as I would have you think,

That had in it a crannied hole or chink,

Through which the lovers, Pyramus and Thisby,   **160**

Did whisper often very secretly.

    (*Indicating his costume.*)

This loam, this rough-cast, and this stone doth

    show

That I am that same wall; the truth is so.

    (*Holding up two fingers.*)

And this the cranny is, right and sinister,*   **left**

Through which the fearful* lovers are to whisper.   **fear-filled**

THESEUS.

Would you desire lime and hair to speak better?

DEMETRIUS.

It is the wittiest partition that ever I heard dis-

course, my lord.

    (PYRAMUS [BOTTOM] *enters.*)

THESEUS.

Pyramus draws near the wall. Silence!   **170**

PYRAMUS (BOTTOM).

O grim-looked night! O night with hue so black!

    O night, which ever art when day is not!

O night, O night! Alack, alack, alack,

    I fear my Thisby's promise is forgot!

And thou, O wall, O sweet, O lovely wall,
That stand'st between her father's ground and
mine!
Thou wall, O wall, O sweet and lovely wall,
Show me thy chink, to blink through with mine
eyne!
(WALL [SNOUT] *holds up his fingers.*)
Thanks, courteous wall. Jove shield thee well for
this!
But what see I? No Thisby do I see.   180
O wicked wall, through whom I see no bliss!
Cursed be thy stones for thus deceiving me!

THESEUS.

The wall, methinks, being sensible,* should curse ^{able to feel}
again.

PYRAMUS (BOTTOM) (*to the* DUKE, *stepping out of*
character).

No, in truth, sir, he should not. "Deceiving me"
is Thisby's cue: she is to enter now, and I am to
spy her through the wall. You shall see, it will fall
pat as I told you. Yonder she comes.
(THISBE [FLUTE] *enters, on the other side of*
WALL [SNOUT].)

THISBE (FLUTE).

O wall, full often hast thou heard my moans,   190
For parting my fair Pyramus and me!
My cherry lips have often kissed thy stones,
Thy stones with lime and hair knit up in thee.

PYRAMUS (BOTTOM).

   I see a voice: now will I to the chink,

   To spy an I can hear my Thisby's face.

     (*Speaking through* WALL'S [SNOUT'S] *fingers.*)

   Thisby!

THISBE (FLUTE) (*speaking through* WALL'S [SNOUT'S]

    fingers).

   My love thou art, my love I think.

PYRAMUS (BOTTOM).

   Think what thou wilt, I am thy lover's grace;

   And, like Limander,* am I trusty still.   *i.e.,* Leander

THISBE (FLUTE).

   And I like Helen,* till the Fates me kill.   *i.e.,* Hero

PYRAMUS (BOTTOM).

   Not Shafalus to Procrus was so true.[60]   200

THISBE (FLUTE).

   As Shafalus to Procrus, I to you.

PYRAMUS (BOTTOM).

   O, kiss me through the hole of this vile wall!

THISBE (FLUTE) (*kissing*).

   I kiss the wall's hole, not your lips at all.

PYRAMUS (BOTTOM).

   Wilt thou at Ninny's tomb meet me straightway?

THISBE (FLUTE).

   'Tide life, 'tide death,* I come without delay.   Come life, come death

    (PYRAMUS [BOTTOM] *and* THISBE [FLUTE] *go.*)

WALL (SNOUT) (*stepping forward*).
   Thus have I, Wall, my part dischargèd so;
   And, being done, thus Wall away doth go.
      (*Bowing, he exits.*)

THESEUS.
   Now is the mural* down between the two neigh-   wall
   bors.   210

DEMETRIUS.
   No remedy, my lord, when walls are so willful to
   hear without warning.

HIPPOLYTA.
   This is the silliest stuff that ever I heard.

THESEUS.
   The best in this kind are but shadows; and the
   worst are no worse, if imagination amend them.

HIPPOLYTA.
   It must be your imagination then, and not theirs.

THESEUS.
   If we imagine no worse of them than they of them-
   selves, they may pass for excellent men.
      (LION [SNUG] *and* MOONSHINE [STARVELING]
      enter.)
   Here come two noble beasts in, a man and a lion.   220

LION (SNUG) (*stepping forward*).
   You, ladies, you whose gentle hearts do fear
      The smallest monstrous mouse that creeps on
        floor,

May now perchance both quake and tremble here,
   When lion rough in wildest rage doth roar.
Then know that I, one Snug the joiner, am
A lion-fell,* nor else no lion's dam;[61]   lionskin
For, if I should as lion come in strife
Into this place, 'twere pity on my life.   **230**

THESEUS.
  A very gentle beast, and of a good conscience.

DEMETRIUS.
  The very best at a beast, my lord, that e'er I saw.

LYSANDER.
  This lion is a very fox for his valor.

THESEUS.
  True; and a goose for his discretion.

DEMETRIUS.
  Not so, my lord; for his valor cannot carry his discretion; and the fox carries the goose.

THESEUS.
  His discretion, I am sure, cannot carry his valor;   **240**
for the goose carries not the fox. It is well: leave
it to his discretion, and let us listen to the moon.

MOONSHINE (STARVELING) (*stepping forward and
    holding up his lanthorn*).
  This lanthorn* doth the hornèd moon present—   lantern

DEMETRIUS.
  He should have worn the horns on his head.[62]

THESEUS.
  He is no crescent, and his horns are invisible within

the circumference.

MOONSHINE (STARVELING).

This lanthorn doth the hornèd moon present;
Myself the man i' the moon do seem to be.

THESEUS.

This is the greatest error of all the rest: the man   250
should be put into the lanthorn. How is it else the
man i' the moon?

DEMETRIUS.

He dares not come there for the candle; for, you
see, it is already in snuff.*63   anger

HIPPOLYTA.

I am aweary of this moon. Would he would
change!

THESEUS.

It appears, by his small light of discretion, that he
is in the wane; but yet, in courtesy, in all reason,
we must stay the time.*   *i.e.,* see it
                                                             through
LYSANDER.

Proceed, Moon.   260

MOONSHINE (STARVELING).

All that I have to say, is, to tell you that the
lanthorn is the moon; I, the man in the moon; this
thorn-bush, my thorn-bush; and this dog, my dog.

DEMETRIUS.

Why, all these should be in the lanthorn; for all
these are in the moon. (THISBE [FLUTE] *enters*.)
But, silence! Here comes Thisbe.

THISBE (FLUTE).

This is old Ninny's tomb. Where is my love?

LION (SNUG) (*roaring*).

Oh——

(THISBE [FLUTE] *runs away, dropping her mantle.*)

DEMETRIUS.

Well roared, Lion.

270

THESEUS.

Well run, Thisbe.

HIPPOLYTA.

Well shone, Moon. Truly, the moon shines with a good grace.

(LION [SNUG] *takes* THISBE'S [FLUTE'S] *mantle in his mouth, shakes it, and leaves.*)

THESEUS.

Well moused, Lion.

LYSANDER.

And so the lion vanished.

DEMETRIUS.

And then came Pyramus.

(PYRAMUS [BOTTOM] *enters.*)

PYRAMUS (BOTTOM).

Sweet Moon, I thank thee for thy sunny beams;
  I thank thee, Moon, for shining now so bright;
For, by thy gracious, golden, glittering gleams,
  I trust to take of truest Thisby sight.

280

(*Seeing* THISBE'S [FLUTE'S] *mantle.*)

But stay, O spite!
But mark, poor knight,
What dreadful dole* is here!   grief
Eyes, do you see?
How can it be?
O dainty duck! O dear!
Thy mantle good,
What, stained with blood!
Approach, ye Furies fell!*⁶⁴   fierce
O Fates, come, come,⁶⁵   290
Cut thread and thrum;⁶⁶
Quail,* crush, conclude, and quell!*   subdue/
                                                                    kill

THESEUS.

This passion, and the death of a dear friend, would
go near to make a man look sad.

HIPPOLYTA.

Beshrew my heart, but I pity the man.

PYRAMUS (BOTTOM).

O wherefore, Nature, didst thou lions frame?
Since lion vile hath here deflowered my dear:
Which is—no, no—which was the fairest dame
That lived, that loved, that liked, that looked
with cheer.
Come, tears, confound;   300
(*Drawing his sword.*)
Out, sword, and wound
The pap of Pyramus;

Ay, that left pap,
Where heart doth hop.
(*Stabs himself.*)
Thus die I, thus, thus, thus.
(*Slowly falls.*)
Now am I dead,
Now am I fled;
My soul is in the sky:
Tongue, lose thy light;
Moon, take thy flight.   310
(MOONSHINE [STARVELING] *goes.*)
Now die, die, die, die, die.
(PYRAMUS [BOTTOM] *dies.*)

DEMETRIUS.

No die, but an ace,[67] for him; for he is but one.

LYSANDER.

Less than an ace, man; for he is dead; he is nothing.

THESEUS.

With the help of a surgeon he might yet recover,
and prove an ass.

HIPPOLYTA.

How chance Moonshine is gone before Thisbe
comes back and finds her lover?

THESEUS.

She will find him by starlight. Here she comes;   320
and her passion ends the play.

(THISBE [FLUTE] *returns.*)

HIPPOLYTA.

Methinks she should not use a long one for such a
Pyramus: I hope she will be brief.

DEMETRIUS.

A mote will turn the balance, which Pyramus,
which Thisbe, is the better; he for a man, God
warrant us; she for a woman, God bless us.

(THISBE [FLUTE] *discovers* PYRAMUS [BOTTOM].)

LYSANDER.

She hath spied him already with those sweet eyes.

DEMETRIUS.

And thus she means,* videlicet: laments

THISBE (FLUTE).

Asleep, my love?   331
What, dead, my dove?
O Pyramus, arise!
Speak, speak. Quite dumb?
Dead, dead? A tomb
Must cover thy sweet eyes.
These lily lips,
This cherry nose,
These yellow cowslip cheeks,
Are gone, are gone: 340
Lovers, make moan:
His eyes were green as leeks.
O Sisters Three,*   *i.e.,* the Fates
Come, come to me,
With hands as pale as milk;

Lay them in gore,
Since you have shore
With shears his thread of silk.
Tongue, not a word:
(*Taking up* PYRAMUS' [BOTTOM'S] *sword.*)
Come, trusty sword;   350
Come, blade, my breast imbrue:*   stain with
blood
(*Stabs herself.*)
And, farewell, friends;
Thus Thisbe ends:
Adieu, adieu, adieu.
(THISBE [FLUTE] *dies.*)

THESEUS.

Moonshine and Lion are left to bury the dead.

DEMETRIUS.

Ay, and Wall too.

BOTTOM (*rising quickly*).

No, I assure you; the wall is down that parted
their fathers. Will it please you to see the epilogue, or to hear a Bergomask dance⁶⁸ between   360
two of our company?

THESEUS.

No epilogue, I pray you; for your play needs no
excuse. Never excuse; for when the players are all
dead, there need none to be blamed. Marry, if he
that writ it had played Pyramus and hanged himself in Thisbe's garter, it would have been a fine

tragedy. And so it is, truly; and very notably dis-
charged. But, come, your Bergomask. Let your
epilogue alone.

(*The characters in the play return, perform a
dance, and leave.*)

The iron tongue of midnight hath told twelve: 370

(*To the assembled company.*)

Lovers, to bed; 'tis almost fairy time.
I fear we shall outsleep the coming morn
As much as we this night have overwatched.
This palpable-gross* play hath well beguiled   crude
The heavy gait of night.

                    Sweet friends, to bed.
A fortnight hold we this solemnity,
In nightly revels and new jollity.

(THESEUS *and* HIPPOLYTA, LYSANDER *and* HERMIA,
DEMETRIUS *and* HELENA, *and all* LORDS *and* AT-
TENDANTS *leave. After a moment,* PUCK *enters.*)

PUCK.

Now the hungry lion roars,
  And the wolf behowls the moon;
Whilst the heavy plowman snores,   380
  All with weary task fordone.*   worn out
Now the wasted brands do glow,
  Whilst the screech-owl, screeching loud,
Puts the wretch that lies in woe
  In remembrance of a shroud.

Now it is the time of night
  That the graves all gaping wide,
Every one lets forth his sprite,
  In the church-way paths to glide:
And we fairies, that do run   390
  By the triple Hecate's team,[69]
From the presence of the sun,
  Following darkness like a dream,
Now are frolic.* Not a mouse   frolicsome
Shall disturb this hallowed house:
I am sent with broom before,
To sweep the dust behind the door.[70]
  (OBERON *and* TITANIA *enter, followed by their*
  train of FAIRIES.)

OBERON.

Through the house give glimmering light,
  By the dead and drowsy fire:
Every elf and fairy sprite   400
  Hop as light as bird from brier;
And this ditty, after me,
Sing, and dance it trippingly.

TITANIA.

First, rehearse your song by rote,
To each word a warbling note:
Hand in hand, with fairy grace,
Will we sing, and bless this place.
  (*Music is heard, and all the* FAIRIES *dance.*)

OBERON.

Now, until the break of day,
Through this house each fairy stray.
To the best bride-bed will we,　　　　　　　　410
Which by us shall blessèd be;
And the issue there create*　　　　　　　　created
Ever shall be fortunate.
So shall all the couples three
Ever true in loving be;
And the blots of Nature's hand
Shall not in their issue stand;
Never mole, hare lip, nor scar,
Nor mark prodigious,* such as are　　　　　unnatural
Despised in nativity,　　　　　　　　　　420
Shall upon their children be.
With this field-dew consecrate,*　　　　　consecrated
Every fairy take his gait;
And each several* chamber bless,　　　　　separate
Through this palace, with sweet peace;
And the owner of it blest
Ever shall in safety rest.
Trip away; make no stay;
Meet me all by break of day.

　　　(OBERON, TITANIA, *and the train of* FAIRIES *leave.*)

PUCK.

If we shadows have offended,　　　　　　430
Think but this, and all is mended,
That you have but slumbered here

While these visions did appear.
And this weak and idle theme,
No more yielding but a dream,
Gentles,* do not reprehend,

i.e., ladies
and gentlemen

If you pardon, we will mend.
And, as I am an honest Puck,
If we have unearnèd luck
Now to 'scape the serpent's tongue,

440

We will make amends ere long,
Else the Puck a liar call.
So, good night unto you all.
Give me your hands, if we be friends,
And Robin shall restore amends.

(*He goes.*)

Selected Commentaries

WILLIAM HAZLITT (1778–1830)

Hazlitt's view of *A Midsummer Night's Dream* is like that of other critics of the romantic movement. After showing how true to nature, in the subtlest sense of the word, are the characters and their actions, Hazlitt explains that all that is finest in the comedy is lost when it is played on the stage. Few, if any, critics since his day take this view. The great and continued popularity of the comedy on the stage is an effective answer to the opinion of the romantics.

THE DIMINUTION OF THE NATURE OF THE CHARACTERS THROUGH THEIR APPEARANCE ON THE STAGE
(from: *The Characters of Shakespeare's Plays*, 1817)

Bottom the Weaver is a character that has not had justice done him. He is the most romantic of mechanics. And what a list of companions he has—Quince the Carpenter, Snug the Joiner, Flute the Bellows Mender, Snout the Tinker, Starveling the Tailor; and then again, what a group of fairy attendants, Puck, Peaseblossom, Cobweb, Moth, and Mustardseed! It has been observed that Shakespear's characters are constructed upon deep physiological principles; and there is something in this play which looks very like it. Bottom the Weaver, who takes the lead of

> This crew of patches, rude mechanicals,
> That work for bread upon Athenian stalls,

follows a sedentary trade, and he is accordingly represented as conceited, serious, and fantastical. He is ready to undertake anything and everything, as if it was as much a matter of course as the motion of his loom and shuttle. He is for playing the tyrant, the lover, the lady, the lion. "He will roar that it shall do any man's heart good to hear him"; and this being objected to as improper, he still has a resource in his good opinion of himself, and "will roar you an 'twere any nightingale." Snug the Joiner is the moral man of the piece, who proceeds by measurement and discretion in all things. You see him with his rule and compasses in his hand. "Have you the lion's part written? Pray you, if it be, give it me, for I am slow of study."—"You may do it extempore," says Quince, "for it is nothing but roaring." Starveling the Tailor keeps the peace, and objects to the lion and the drawn sword. "I believe we must leave the killing out when all's done." Starveling, however, does not start the objections himself, but seconds them when made by others, as if he had not spirit to express his fears without encouragement. It is too much to suppose all this intentional: but it very luckily falls out so. Nature includes all that is implied in the most subtle analytical distinctions; and the same distinctions will be found in Shakespear. Bottom, who is not only chief actor, but stage manager for the occasion, has a device to obviate the danger of frightening the ladies: "Write me a prologue, and let the prologue seem to say, we will do no harm with our swords, and that Pyramus is not killed indeed; and for better assurance, tell that that I, Pyramus, am not Pyramus, but Bottom the Weaver: this will put them out of fear." Bottom seems to have understood the subject of dramatic illusion at least as well as any modern essayist. If our holiday mechanic rules the roost among his follows, he is no less at home in his new character of an ass, "with amiable cheeks, and fair large ears." He instinctively acquires a most learned taste, and grows fastidious in the choice of dried peas and bottled hay. He is quite familiar with his new attendants, and assigns them their parts with all due gravity. "Monsieur Cobweb, good Monsieur, get your weapon in your hand, and kill me a red-hipt humblebee on the top of a thistle, and, good Monsieur, bring me the honey bag." What an exact knowledge is here shown of natural history!

Puck, or Robin Goodfellow, is the leader of the fairy band. He is the Ariel of the *Midsummer Night's Dream;* and yet as unlike as can be to the Ariel in *The Tempest*. No other poet could have made two such different characters out of the same fanciful materials and situations. Ariel is a minister of retribution, who is touched with the sense of pity at the woes he inflicts. Puck is a madcap sprite, full of wantonness and mischief, who laughs at those whom he misleads—"Lord, what fools these mortals be!" Ariel cleaves the air, and executes his mission with the zeal of a winged messenger; Puck is borne along on his fairy errand like the light and glittering gossamer before the breeze. He is, indeed, a most Epicurean little gentleman, dealing in quaint devices, and faring in dainty delights. Prospero and his world of spirits are a set of moralists: but with Oberon and his fairies we are launched at once into the empire of the butterflies. How beautifully is this race of beings contrasted with the men and women actors in the scene, by a single epithet which Titania gives to the latter, "the human mortals!" It is astonishing that Shakespear should be considered, not only by foreigners, but by many of our own critics, as a gloomy and heavy writer, who painted nothing by "gorgons and hydras, and chimeras dire." His subtlety exceeds that of all other dramatic writers, insomuch that a celebrated person of the present day said that he regarded him rather as a metaphysician than a poet. His delicacy and sportive gaiety are infinite. In the *Midsummer Night's Dream* alone, we should imagine, there is more sweetness and beauty of description than in the whole range of French poetry put together. What we mean is this, that we will produce out of that single play ten passages, to which we do not think any ten passages in the works of the French poets can be opposed, displaying equal fancy and imagery. Shall we mention the remonstrance of Helena to Hermia, or Titania's description of her fairy train, or her disputes with Oberon about the Indian boy, or Puck's account of himself and his employments, or the Fairy Queen's exhortation to the elves to pay due attendance upon her favorite, Bottom; or Hippolita's description of a chase, or Theseus's answer? The two last are as heroical and spirited as the others are full of luscious tenderness. The reading of this play is like wandering in a grove by moonlight: the descriptions breathe a sweetness like odors thrown from beds of flowers.

Titania's exhortation to the fairies to wait upon Bottom, which is remarkable for a certain cloying sweetness in the repetition of the rhymes, is as follows:

> Be kind and courteous to this gentleman.
> Hop in his walks, and gambol in his eyes,
> Feed him with apricocks and dewberries,
> With purple grapes, green figs and mulberries;
> The honey bags steal from the humblebees,
> And for night tapers crop their waxen thighs,
> And light them at the fiery glowworm's eyes,
> To have my love to bed, and to arise:
> And pluck the wings from painted butterflies,
> To fan the moonbeams from his sleeping eyes;
> Nod to him, elves, and do him courtesies.

The sounds of the lute and of the trumpet are not more distinct than the poetry of the foregoing passage, and of the conversation between Theseus and Hippolita.

> *Theseus.* Go, one of you, find out the forester,
>   For now our observation is perform'd;
>   And since we have the vaward of the day,
>   My love shall hear the music of my hounds.
>   Uncouple in the western valley, go,
>   Dispatch, I say, and find the forester.
>   We will, fair Queen, up to the mountain's top,
>   And mark the musical confusion
>   Of hounds and echo in conjunction.

> *Hippolyta.* I was with Hercules and Cadmus once,
>   When in a wood of Crete they bay'd the bear
>   With hounds of Sparta; never did I hear
>   Such gallant chiding. For besides the groves,
>   The skies, the fountains, every region near
>   Seem'd all one mutual cry. I never heard

So musical a discord, such sweet thunder.

Theseus. My hounds are bred out of the Spartan kind,
So flew'd, so sanded, and their heads are hung
With ears that sweep away the morning dew;
Crook-knee'd and dew-lap'd, like Thessalian bulls.
Slow in pursuit, but matched in mouth like bells,
Each under each. A cry more tunable
Was never halloo'd to, nor cheer'd with horn,
In Crete, in Sparta, nor in Thessaly:
Judge when you hear.

Even Titian never made a hunting piece of a *gusto* so fresh and lusty, and so near the first ages of the world as this.

It had been suggested to us, that the *Midsummer Night's Dream* would do admirably to get up as a Christmas afterpiece; and our prompter proposed that Mr. Kean should play the part of Bottom, as worthy of his great talents. He might, in the discharge of his duty, offer to play the lady like any of our actresses that he pleased, the lover or the tyrant like any of our actors that he pleased, and the lion like "the most fearful wildfowl living." The carpenter, the tailor, and joiner, it was thought, would hit the galleries. The young ladies in love would interest the side boxes; and Robin Goodfellow and his companions excite a lively fellow feeling in the children from school. There would be two courts, an empire within an empire, the Athenian and the Fairy King and Queen, with their attendants, and with all their finery. What an opportunity for processions, for the sound of trumpets and glittering of spears! What a fluttering of urchins' painted wings; what a delightful profusion of gauze clouds and airy spirits floating on them!

Alas the experiment has been tried, and has failed; not through the fault of Mr. Kean, who did not play the part of Bottom, nor of Mr. Liston, who did, and who played it well, but from the nature of things. The *Midsummer Night's Dream*, when acted, is converted from a delightful fiction into a dull pantomime. All that is finest in the play is lost in the representation. The spectacle was grand: but the spirit was evaporated, the genius was fled. Poetry and the stage do not agree well together. The attempt to reconcile them in this instance fails not only of effect, but of decorum. The *ideal* can have no place upon the stage, which is a picture without perspective; everything there is in the foreground. That which was merely an airy shape, a dream, a passing thought, immediately becomes an unmanageable reality. Where all is left to the imagination (as is the case in reading) every circumstance, near or remote, has an equal chance of being kept in mind, and tells according to the mixed impression of all that has been suggested. But the imagination cannot sufficiently qualify the actual impressions of the senses. Any offense given to the eye is not to be got rid of by explanation. Thus Bottom's head in the play is a fantastic illusion, produced by magic spells: on the stage it is an ass's head, and nothing more; certainly a very strange costume for a gentleman to appear in. Fancy cannot be embodied any more than a simile can be painted; and it is as idle to attempt it as to personate *Wall* or *Moonshine*. Fairies are not incredible, but fairies six feet high are so. Monsters are not shocking, if they are seen at a proper distance. When ghosts appear at midday, when apparitions stalk along Cheapside, then may the *Midsummer Night's Dream* be represented without injury at Covent Garden or at Drury Lane. The boards of a theater and the regions of fancy are not the same thing.

* * *

FREDERICK JAMES FURNIVALL (1825–1910)

Furnivall was among the greatest and most influential English scholars of the nineteenth century. He was one of the founders of the Oxford English Dictionary, of the English Text Society, and of the New Shakespeare Society, many of whose texts he edited. While he devoted most of his scholarly activity to Chaucer, two books on Shakespeare are notable: Shakespeare's *Life and Work*, 1908, and the editorship, in 1877, of the "Leopold" *Shakespeare*, a limited and beautifully illustrated edition of the plays presented in their chronological order.

EVIDENCE OF THE EARLY COMPOSITION OF THE PLAY
(from: Introduction to the "Leopold" *Shakespeare*, 1877)

The fairies are the centre of the drama; the human characters are just the sport of their whims and fancies, a fact which is much altered when we come to Shakspere's use of fairy-land again in his *Tempest*, where the aërial beings are but ministers of the wise man's rule for the highest purposes. The finest character here is undoubtedly Theseus. In his noble words about the countrymen's play, the true gentleman is shown. His wife's character is but poor beside his. Though the story is Greek, yet the play is full of English life. It is Stratford which has given Shakspere the picture of the sweet country school girls working at one flower, warbling one song, growing together like a double cherry, seeming parted, but yet a union in partition. It is Stratford that has given him the picture of the hounds with 'Ears that sweep away the morning dew.' It is Stratford that has given him his out-door woodland life, his clowns' play, and the clowns themselves, Bottom, with his inimitable conceit, and his fellows, Snug and Quince, &c. It is Stratford that has given him all Puck's fairy-lore, the cowslips tall, the red-hipt bumble bee, Oberon's bank, the pansy love-in-idleness, and all the lovely imagery of the play. But wonderful as the mixture of delicate and aërial fancy with the coarsest and broadest comedy is, clearly as it evidences the coming of a new being on this earth to whom anything is possible, it is yet clear that the play is quite young. The undignified quarreling of the ladies, Hermia with her 'painted May-pole,' her threat to scratch Helena's eyes,— Helena with her retorts 'She was a vixen when she went to school,' &c., the comical comparison of the moon tumbling through the earth (III, ii, 52) incongruously put into an accusation of murder, the descent to bathos in Shakspere's passage about his own art, from 'the poet's eye in a fine frenzy roll-ing' to 'how easy is a bush supposed a bear,' would have been impossible to Shakspere in his later developement. Those who contend for the later date of the play, from the beauty of most of the fancy, and the allusion to the effects of the rains and the floods, which they make those of 1594, must allow, I think, that the framework of the play is considerably before the date of *King John* and *The Merchant of Venice*. Possibly two dates may be allowed for the play, tho' I don't think them needful. . . .

With the *Dream* I propose to close the first Group of Shakspere's Comedies, those in which the Errors arising from mistaken identity make so much of the fun. And the name of the group may well be 'the Comedy of Errors or Mistaken-Identity Group.'

* * *

THOMAS M. PARROTT (1866–1960)

Thomas M. Parrott was for many years a Professor of English at Princeton University, whose field of specialization was the Elizabethan drama. His books were written for students rather than for scholars. His principal works are *The Problem of Timon of Athens* (1923), *Shakespearean Comedy* (1948), *William Shakespeare, a Handbook* (rev. ed., 1953), and *A Short View of Elizabethan Drama* (1958).

In the following excerpt, Parrott relates *A Midsummer Night's Dream* to the poet's earlier comedies and to those of some of his contemporaries. He stresses, in particular, Bottom's development of the conventional clown, which endows him with just those qualities needed to hold into unity the three fantastic worlds out of which the poet has constructed his comedy.

THE RELATION OF THE FORM AND CHARACTERS OF *A Midsummer Night's Dream* TO THE POET'S EARLIER WORK AND THAT OF HIS PREDECESSORS
(from: *Shakespearean Comedy*, 1948)

In spite of the absence of a source or pattern to work from, Shakespeare produced in *A Midsummer Night's Dream* what his two immediately preceding comedies had lacked, a coherent and interesting action. The contrast with the almost plotless *Love's Labour's Lost* is remarkable, and the neat solution of the intrigue, first induced and then resolved by magic, is an immense improvement on the hurried and unsatisfactory denouement of *The Two Gentlemen*. The action starts promptly in the first scene and runs its course unbroken to the close of the fourth act. The last act, devoted almost entirely to the Pyramus and Thisbe interlude, serves in a measure to bring us back to earth again after a night in the fairies' enchanted wood. That the main action is in the highest degree improbable does not make it the less entertaining. Like Lyly's *Woman in the Moon* 'all is but a poet's dream,' as, in fact, the very title tells us; yet the characters that move through this dream are more substantial flesh and blood than any of Lyly's shadowy figures.

It would be absurd to equate Shakespeare's power of characterization in this play with that shown at the height of his career. Yet one has only to compare the Duke of the *Dream* with Duke Solinus of *The Comedy of Errors* to see Shakespeare's advance in this phase of his art. Both belong to the enveloping action; neither has an essential part in the main plot; but here the likeness ends. Solinus is a mere puppet, wholly lacking individuality; Theseus, on the contrary, is a firmly realized figure, a soldier, a sportsman, breeding hounds 'of the Spartan kind,' like an English squire, and a lover, whose sane and sensible affection contrasts, as Shakespeare meant it to do, with the fickle fancy of the lovers. A man of action rather than of sentiment, Theseus is a little contemptuous of the fine frenzy of the poet, but like a courteous Tudor prince he is ready to accept whatever entertainment his subjects offer him, whether the 'premeditated welcomes' of great clerks which broke down half-spoken, or the homely shows of rustics; for, says he,

> Never anything can be amiss,
> When simpleness and duty tender it.

Shakespeare refrained from characterizing sharply the two gentlemen of the main plot; to have done so would have defeated his purpose in showing them the helpless victims of the fairy charm. Of the ladies an anonymous critic, quoted by Cunningham in his edition of this play, remarks that Helena and Hermia differ only in height. They do, indeed, so differ. Evidently Shakespeare found in his company two boys for these rôles, one tall and slender, one short and plump, and he cleverly exploited these physical differences. But only wilfully blinded criticism can fail to distinguish between the warm-hearted, quick-tempered, little Hermia and her tall, sentimental, spaniel-like friend. The ladies, we may note, never come under the love spell, and accordingly it was possible for Shakespeare to endow them with more individual and distinguishing characteristics than he could allow their lovers. There is a delightfully feminine touch in Helena's appeal to the men for protection against the physical violence threatened by her former playmate, who 'was a vixen when she went to school.'

Shakespeare's supreme piece of character portrayal in the *Dream* is the figure of Bully Bottom. This is, of course, a clown's role for Kempe and by far the best that Shakespeare had yet composed for him. For Bottom, while he retains many of the Clown's old tricks, develops into something much more than a mere clown. He is one of the eternally comic figures of literature, not a country bumpkin like his predecessor Costard, but the perennial 'life-of-the-party' in a small town, cheery, loquacious, conceited, and unabashed. Although a prominent figure in a romantic comedy, there is not a trace of romantic sentiment in Bottom. Modern psychology would, perhaps, classify him as a pragmatist, for he meets each situation as it arises with complete self-confidence. Cast for the part of a lover he promptly offers to play the lady's part, or the lion's, though his chief humor is for a tyrant, a part to 'tear a cat in,' 'a lover is more condoling.' Abandoned by his comrades and alone in the haunted wood at night, he sings and jests to show that he is not afraid. Courted by the Queen of Fairyland he has no sense of the glamor and the danger of his situation—for that we must turn to the old ballad of *Thomas the Rymer*. Bottom accepts the kisses of his fairy mistress with the utmost complacency and calls for a 'bottle of hay' and the music of tongs and bones. Incongruity is one of the essentials of the comic and there is no more incongruous situation in literature than that of Bottom with his 'fair large ears' asleep in the arms of the dainty Titania. Romance and realism are here contrasted and combined.

A Midsummer Night's Dream has never enjoyed great success upon the stage, but it is one of the most delightful of Shakespeare's plays for the closet. The diction of this play, less marred by fanciful conceits than that of earlier comedies, less obscured by involved passages where thought seems to wrestle with expression as in later and greater plays, offers a constant source of enjoyment to the reader. Through the simple medium of language without the charm of theatrical illusion, Shakespeare tells an interesting story of human lovers and opens to the imaginative reader the magic gates of fairyland. It is in his use of language, as in so much else in this play, that Shakespeare shows himself the master. There is a fair proportion of prose, strictly reserved for the realistic talk of Bottom and his fellows. Bottom's lines, in particular, have been most carefully written; Shakespeare seems determined to prevent his clown in this play from speaking more than was set down for him. Kempe had no chance in the *Dream* to address the audience directly as he had done in the role of Launce, or to work impromptus into the dialogue, as he seems to have done during the rehearsals of *Love's Labour's Lost*. Modern readers can enjoy Bottom's chatter without trying to visualize Kempe's jigs.

Over half the verse lines of the *Dream* are in rhyme. The 'jigging vein' of the Pyramus play is Shakespeare's mockery of the 'mother wits' who wrote plays before the new group of playwrights, Peele, Marlowe, and Greene, established blank verse and rhymed iambic couplets on the stage. The lovers, for the most part, speak in rhyme, which is as it should be, but Shakespeare restrains here the exuberance that had flourished so freely in *Love's Labour's Lost;* there are no sonnets embodied in the dialogue of the *Dream*. The extravagant language of Lysander and Demetrius, awaking after their eyes had been touched by the love juice, is purposely designed to show the power of that spell; they do not rant in this vein either before or after.

The blank verse of the *Dream* is distinguished at once by ease and beauty; there is little or no rhetorical declamation in this play. Shakespeare has gained full control over the meter he had learned to use from Marlowe, and has put something new into it, a lyric quality of tone. The fairy scenes seem to have been written to music: Shakespeare, it is clear, was able to command for the first performance a group of singing boys whose fresh voices ring out in solo, recitative, and chorus. Their songs, naturally and rightly, are in rhyme, but even in the regular blank verse speeches of Oberon and Titania the lyric note is heard. Take, for example, two passages of many that might be culled from this fair garden, Oberon's words to Puck:

> But I might see young Cupid's fiery shaft
> Quench'd in the chaste beams of the wat'ry moon,
> And the imperial votaress passed on,
> In maiden meditation, fancy-free.
> Yet mark'd I where the bolt of Cupid fell:
> It fell upon a little western flower,
> Before milk-white, now purple with love's wound,
> And maidens call it, Love-in-idleness

or Titania's order to her attendant elves:

> Come, now a roundel and a fairy song;
> Then, for the third part of a minute, hence;
> Some to kill cankers in the musk-rose buds,
> Some war with rere-mice for their leathern wings
> To make my small elves coats, and some keep back
> The clamorous owl, that nightly hoots, and wonders

At our quaint spirits. . .

The distinguishing characteristic of the *Dream*, in fact, is that it attains what *The Two Gentlemen* had aimed at and failed to achieve: lyric romantic comedy. Shakespeare was to do still better work than this; he had not yet mastered all the stops of his organ, but there is a gay and youthful freshness in the music of this play that makes it a joy forever. It was surely of the *Dream* that Milton was thinking when he spoke of Shakespeare warbling 'his native wood-notes wild.'

There is something more, of course, in *A Midsummer Night's Dream* than Shakespeare's wood-notes. The central action is concerned with that phase of human love which the Elizabethans called 'fancy': the irrational emotional impulse that draws man to maid and maid to man. Love as 'fancy,' 'love-in-idleness,' is a conception of love proper to comedy, and this early comedy plays with it and exhibits its most fantastic form in Titania's infatuation. Shakespeare's mastery of his art permits him here to sport with his theme in easy good humor. Like Puck he is vastly entertained by human follies. 'What fools these mortals be' might serve as a second title for the play, but there is nothing satirical or malicious in the playwright's laughter. The shadow of death or danger that hangs over his earlier comedies, and was to reappear in still darker shades hereafter, has vanished in the enchanted moonlight that floods the wood near Athens. Nowhere in all Shakespeare's work do we hear him singing in so carefree a strain as in *A Midsummer Night's Dream*.

*   *   *

ENID WELSFORD

Enid Welsford was educated at University College, London, and at Newnham College of Cambridge University. In 1927 she was appointed Lecturer in English at Newnham, and in 1928, Lecturer in the Faculty of English at Cambridge University. Also, in 1928, she was awarded a prize by the British Academy for her book *The Court Masque* (1927). A more recent work is *The Fool, His Social and Literary History* (1958). Miss Welsford is now retired from her college and university lectureships, but continues to teach occasionally at the various Cambridge colleges.

In the following excerpt, Miss Welsford argues that Shakespeare, instead of endowing his comedy with the actual body of the masque, has transmuted its characteristic features of music, carpentry, dancing, and scenic splendor into poetry that weaves all of them into a finely wrought structure. Bottom and his companions serve the purpose of the antimasque, a grotesque action introduced for the sake of sharp contrast to the gorgeous display of the masque proper.

THE INFLUENCE OF THE MASQUE UPON *A Midsummer Night's Dream*
(from: *The Court Masque*, 1927)

For the question as to the relation between *A Midsummer Night's Dream*, *The Tempest*, and the court masque, is not merely a matter of classification: behind it lies the vital question as to how far the art of a nation is dependent on the quantity and quality of its recreation, and how far the individual genius is dependent upon the artistic talent diffused throughout society.

The suggestion that *A Midsummer Night's Dream* and *The Tempest* should be regarded as masques has little to recommend it. In all probability both plays were written for the celebration of court weddings, but they are not masques, because there are no masquers, because they are independent of their occasion, because their plots are not mere inductions leading up to masque dances, because there is nothing in them corresponding to the sudden failure of detachment which occurs at the end of Peele's *Arraignment of Paris*, and even to a lesser extent in the final scene of Milton's *Comus*. On the other hand, if they are further removed from the masque form, they are much closer to its spirit than is *Comus*. For Shakespeare perceived, or at any rate acted upon, the principle that the masque must die to live. Ben Jonson failed nobly in his effort to exalt the soul of the masque, because he was forever hampered by its body, but Shakespeare, being a playwright, not a masque poet, was able to disregard the masque body altogether, and instead of having to supply the place of music, carpentry, and dancing by inadequate prose description, he transmuted all these things into poetry, and wove them into the very texture of his plays.

The scenic element is almost as important in *A Midsummer Night's Dream* as in the masque, but it is treated in a very different way. The wood near Athens is not dependent upon, rather it is antagonistic to, the art of the scene painter. Even if *A Midsummer Night's Dream* was well staged at court, still Oberon's description of his surrounding could hardly be translated into terms of paint and canvas, for what scene painter would be quite equal to the "bank where the wild thyme blows," or, indeed, what human actor could obey Titania's stage direction:

> Come, now a roundel and a fairy song;
> Then, for the third part of a minute, hence?

The feeling of the countryside, the romantic fairy-haunted earth has affected the very details of language.

> Your eyes are lodestars; and your tongue's sweet air
> More tunable than lark to shepherd's ear,
> When wheat is green, when hawthorn buds appear.

When Bottom appears with his ass's head:

> As wild geese that the creeping fowler eye,
> Or russet-pated choughs, many in sort,
> Rising and cawing at the gun's report,
> Sever themselves and madly sweep the sky;
> So, at his sight, away his fellows fly.

Titania winds Bottom in her arms:

> So doth the woodbine the sweet honeysuckle
> Gently entwist; the female ivy so
> Enrings the barky fingers of the elm.

"Acorn," "canker blossom," "hindering knot grass," are epithets flung at each other by the quarrelsome lovers.

When Duke Theseus has left the lovers to themselves, Demetrius, still dazed and only half awake, murmurs:

> These things seem small and undistinguishable,
> Like far-off mountains turned into clouds.

It is a fine image, giving just that suggestion of awe and uncertainty which was needed to soften the transition from dream to waking life. The magic of the phrase lies in the words "small" and "undistinguishable." A lesser poet would probably have given the abstract idea in the first line and in the second its concrete illustration. But the word "small" (instead of "strange," "vague" or some other word of that kind) at once sets the imagination to work and suggests the picture which the next line expands, and the sound of the word "undistinguishable," with its accumulated syllables trailing off into silence, does for the ear what the word "small" does for the eye, suggests the shimmering atmosphere, the blurred outline, and the gradual vanishing of the distant mountains on the horizon.

Shakespeare has absorbed the scenic splendor of the masque, not only in description and picturesque language, but also in a blending of tones, a harmony of colors, which the poet has attained by a most delicate and subtle handling of the laws of resemblance and contrast. The play opens in the daylight, first in the court, then in the cottage, and brings us into the presence of the two sets of characters who most emphatically belong to daylight and the solid earth, the genial cultivated rulers, the simple-minded artisans, the former serving as a framework, the latter as a foil to the poetry and moonshine of the dream. The excellence of the workmanship lies in the fact that the framework is organically connected with the picture, for Theseus and Hippolyta are accompanied by Philostrate the Master of the Revels. We are in the world of men, but men are in holiday mood. Ordinary workaday business is set aside, pomp, triumph, and reveling are in the air. Anything may happen. The moon is at once made the topic of conversation:

> Four days will quickly steep themselves in night;
> Four night will quickly dream away the time;
> And then the moon, like to a silver bow
> New-bent in heaven, shall behold the night
> Of our solemnities.

By the end of the first act our minds are full of the wood where Helena and Hermia used to lie "upon faint primrose beds," where the young people used to meet "to do observance to a morn of May," and where very shortly lovers and workmen are to assemble by moonlight for diverse purposes. Moonshine is almost as real a personage in Shakespeare's as in Bottom's play. Her presence permeates the action, a delicate compliment to the maiden Queen, and Titania is merely a glancing beam of her light. Even the workmen help to make her presence felt:

Quince. Well, it shall be so. But there is two hard things, that is, to bring the moonlight into a chamber; for, you know, Pyramus and Thisby meet by moonlight.

Snout. Doth the moon shine that night we play our play?

Bottom. A calendar, a calendar! look in the almanac; find out moonshine, find out moonshine.

Quince. Yes, it doth shine that night.

Bottom. Why, then may you leave a casement of the great chamber window, where we play, open; and the moon may shine in at the casement.

Quince. Ay; or else one must come in with a bush of thorns and a lanthorne and say he comes to disfigure, or to present, the person of Moonshine.

But if the transition from daylight to moonlight is delicately wrought; it is far surpassed by the gradual oncoming of the dawn in Acts III and IV.

The first hint comes when Oberon commands Puck to cover the starry welkin with fog, the better to mislead the angry lovers. The latter replies:

> My fairy lord, this must be done with haste,
> For night's swift dragons cut the clouds full fast,
> And yonder shines Aurora's harbinger.

Then in comes Lysander vainly hunting for Demetrius. Thwarted by the darkness, he lies down to rest:

> Come, thou gentle day!
> For if but once thou show me thy gray light,
> I'll find Demetrius and revenge this spite.

In comes Demetrius in similar mood:

> Thou shalt buy this dear,
> If ever I thy face by daylight see:
> Now, go thy way. Faintness constraineth me
> To measure out my length on this cold bed:
> By day's approach look to be visited.

But the women are suffering even more than the men from that exhaustion and bedraggledness, which is so oppressive in the small hours after a sleepless night:

Re-enter Helena.

Helena. O weary night! O long and tedious night,
   Abate thy hours! Shine, comforts, from the east!
   That I may back to Athens by daylight. . . .

Re-enter Hermia.

Hermia. Never so weary, never so in woe,
   Bedabbled with the dew and torn with briers,
   I can no further crawl, no further go;
   My legs can keep no pace with my desires.
   Here will I rest me till the break of day.
   Heavens shield Lysander, if they mean a fray!

The lovers are all asleep on the flowery bank, when they are joined by Titania, Bottom, and the fairies. Bottom has "an exposition of sleep" come upon him and, as he and the Fairy Queen rest together, Oberon and Puck arrive and conquer Cupid's flower by Dian's bud. Titania wakes, freed from the spell, takes hands with Oberon, and the day dawns.

Puck. Fairy King, attend, and mark:
   I do hear the morning lark.

Oberon. Then, my Queen, in silence sad,
   Trip we after the night's shade;
   We the globe can compass soon,
   Swifter than the wandering moon.

The fairies vanish, a horn winds, Theseus, Hippolyta, and the rest break in with a clatter of horses and hounds, the day breaks, and the shadows flee away. But the broad sunlight is not suited to the Midsummer Night's Dream, the day soon passes and gives place to torchlight. It would have been a simple plan to leave the fairy part in the center of the play as a dream interval in the waking workaday world, but Shakespeare knew better than that. There is nothing more disappointing to a child than to find that the fairy tale was only a dream after all, and children know best how a fairy tale should be conducted.

> The iron tongue of midnight hath tolled twelve;
> Lovers, to bed; 'tis almost fairy time.

Once more the coloring changes. The mortals are gone, the bright festal lights are dimmed, "now the wasted brands do glow," now the fire is dead and drowsy, and very quietly, very lightly, the fairies come in; dreamland has invaded reality, and who shall say which is which, for Puck left behind with his broom and his parting word sweeps the whole thing away, like the leaves of yesteryear.

To compare a very great with a very small thing, the imaginative effect of this kind of plot weaving is like that of the transformation scenes in ballet or pantomime, where groups of dancers come in like waves of color, melting one into another. The effect is attractive even when crudely and unbeautifully designed. Transmuted into poetry, it is of surpassing charm. It could only have been so transmuted at a time when pageantry was part of the people's life, when beauty was an element in all their recreations and "they drew it in as simply as their breath."

Music in the court masque was even more important than scenery. Again and again, in the accounts of Elizabethan and Jacobean revels, we are told of the entrancing quality of the music. Robert Laneham told his merchant friend how Elizabeth stood by night on the bridge at Kenilworth and listened to the music sounding from barges on the quiet water. The music which accompanied the show of the *Lady of the Lake* moved him to ecstasy:

Noow, Syr, the ditty in mitter so aptly endighted to the matter, and after by voys so deliciously deliver'd . . . every instrument agayn in hiz kind so excellently tunabl; and this in the eeving of the day, resoounding from the calm waters, whear prezens of her Majesty, and longing to listen, had utterly damped all noyz and dyn; the hole armony conveyd in tyme, tune, and temper thus incomparably melodious; with what pleazure, Master Martyn, with what sharpnes of conceyt, with what lyvely delighte, this moought pears [pierce] into the heerers harts; I pray ye imagin yoorself az ye may; for, so God judge me, by all the wit and cunning I have, I cannot express, I promis yoo. . . . Muzik iz a nobl art!

This music Shakespeare has transmuted into his poetry, as he has transmuted the spectacular element of pageantry. Laneham's emotion still vibrates in the words of Oberon:

> My gentle Puck, come hither. Thou remember'st
> Since once I sat upon a promontory,
> And heard a mermaid on a dolphin's back
> Uttering such dulcet and harmonious breath,
> That the rude sea grew civil at her song,
> And certain stars shot madly from their spheres,
> To hear the sea maid's music.

The whole play is musically written. It is interesting to compare Milton's famous "Sabrina" lyric with any of the fairy songs in *A Midsummer Night's Dream* and *The Tempest*. In "Sabrina" each word is exquisitely right, each word is an entity with its own peculiar value. In Shakespeare's songs the words melt into one another, and sometimes meaning is almost lost in melody and emotion. There is the same musical quality in the flowing blank verse of *A Midsummer Night's Dream*, verse which is lyrical rather than dramatic; liquid clear, never checked in its course by some sudden, sharp, projecting thought. Milton's dialogue has the terse, stichomythic quality of Greek or Senecan drama, Shakespeare's is a part-song.

The real soul of the masque, however, was the rhythmic movement of living bodies. It is owing to this fact that *A Midsummer Night's Dream* is more nearly related to the genuine masque than is *Comus*. In *Comus*, as we have seen, though dances occur, they are merely incidental, and the play would be scarcely altered by their omission. In *A Midsummer Night's Dream* most—not all—of the dances are vitally connected with the plot. For instance, Titania's awakening in Act IV, Scene i is an important point in the play, for it is the point where the ravel begins to be untangled, and the occasion is celebrated by a dance of reunion between Fairy King and Fairy Queen:

Oberon. Sound, music! Come, my Queen, take hands with me,
   And rock the ground whereon these sleepers be.
   Now thou and I are new in amity.
   And will tomorrow midnight solemnly
   Dance in Duke Theseus' house triumphantly,

And bless it to all fair prosperity.
There shall the pairs of faithful lovers be
Wedded, with Theseus, all in jollity.

The rhythm of the poetry is a dance rhythm, the lines rock and sway with the movement of the fairies. Even more closely in the last scene does the verse echo the light pattering steps of the elves. There is nothing like this in *Comus*. The lyrics there are exquisite, melodious, but they are not dance songs. Even the entry of Comus is poetry of the *Il penseroso* order, imaginative, intellectual, reminiscent, while Shakespeare's lines are alive with movement, and suggest the repeat and turn and rhythmic beat of dancing. In a word, in *Comus* we have thought turned to poetry, while in *A Midsummer Night's Dream* we have sound and movement turned to poetry.

The influence of the dance has affected not merely isolated songs and speeches, but the whole structure of *A Midsummer Night's Dream*. Again a comparison with *Comus* is helpful. The difference in style between *Comus* and *A Midsummer Night's Dream* depends upon a difference of spirit. *Comus* is a criticism of life, it springs from an abstract idea: *A Midsummer Night's Dream* is a dance, a movement of bodies. The plot is a pattern, a figure, rather than a series of events occasioned by human character and passion, and this pattern, especially in the moonlight parts of the play, is the pattern of a dance.

Enter a Fairie at one doore, and Robin Goodfellow at another. . . .
Enter the King of Fairies, at one doore, with his traine; and the

Queene, at another with hers.

The appearance and disappearance and reappearance of the various lovers, the will-o'-the-wisp movement of the elusive Puck, form a kind of figured ballet. The lovers quarrel in a dance pattern: first, there are two men to one woman and the other woman alone, then for a brief space a circular movement, each one pursuing and pursued, then a return to the first figure with the position of the women reversed, then a cross-movement, man quarreling with man and woman with woman, and then, as finale, a general setting to partners, including not only lovers but fairies and royal personages as well.

This dancelike structure makes it inevitable that the lovers should be almost as devoid of character as masquers or masque presenters. The harmony and grace of the action would have been spoiled by convincing passion.

The only character study in *A Midsummer Night's Dream* is to be found in the portrayal of Bottom, Theseus, and perhaps Hippolyta. Even in drawing these characters Shakespeare was evidently influenced by the memory of pageants, complimentary speeches, and entertainments addressed by townspeople and humble folk to the Queen or to the nobility. A glance through Nichols' *Public Progresses* shows what innumerable lengthy speeches, what innumerable disguisings and shows, Elizabeth was obliged to bear with gracious demeanor. Her experiences were similar to those of Theseus:

> Where I have come, great clerks have purposed
> To greet me with premeditated welcomes;
> Where I have seen them shiver and look pale,

Make periods in the midst of sentences,
Throttle their practic'd accent in their fears,
And, in conclusion, dumbly have broke off,
Not paying me a welcome.

One Sunday afternoon, at Kenilworth Castle, Elizabeth and her court whiled away the time by watching the country-people at a Brideale and Morris Dance. Their amused kindly tolerance is just that of Theseus and the lovers towards the Athenian workmen. So that even in the most solid and dramatic parts of his play Shakespeare is only giving an idealized version of courtly and country revels and of the people that played a part in them.

In *A Midsummer Night's Dream* Bottom and his companions serve the same purpose as the antimasque in the courtly revels. It is true that Shakespeare's play was written before Ben Jonson had elaborated and defined the antimasque, but from the first grotesque dances were popular, and the principle of contrast was always latent in the masque. There is, however, a great difference between Jonson's and Shakespeare's management of foil and relief. In the antimasque the transition is sudden and the contrast complete, a method of composition effective enough in spectacle and ballet. But in a play, as Shakespeare well knew, the greatest beauty is gained through contrast when the difference is obvious and striking, but rises out of a deep though unobtrusive resemblance. This could not be better illustrated than by the picture of Titania winding the ass-headed Bottom in her arms. Why is it that this is a pleasing picture, why is it that the rude mechanicals do not, as a matter of fact, disturb or sully Titania's "close and consecrated bower"? Malvolio in Bottom's place would be repellent, yet Malvolio, regarded superficially, is less violently contrasted to the Fairy Queen than is Nick Bottom. Bottom with his ass's head is grotesquely hideous, and in ordinary life he is crude, raw, and very stupid. We have no reason to suppose that Malvolio was anything but a well-set-up, proper-looking man, spruce, well dressed, the perfect family butler. His mentality too is of a distinctly higher order than Bottom's. He fills a responsible position with credit, he follows a reasoned line of conduct, he thinks nobly of the soul. Two things alone he lacks (and that is why no self-respecting fay could ever kiss him)—humor and imagination. Malvolio is, therefore, the only character who cannot be included in the final harmony of *Twelfth Night*. Bottom and his fellows did perhaps lack humor (though the interview with the fairies suggests that Bottom had a smack of it), but in its place they possessed unreason. Imagination they did have, of the most simple, primal, childlike kind. It is their artistic ambition that lifts them out of the humdrum world and turns them into Midsummer Dreamers, and we have seen how cunningly Shakespeare extracts from their very stupidity romance and moonshine. But, indeed, grotesqueness and stupidity (of a certain kind) have a kinship with beauty. For these qualities usually imply a measure of spiritual freedom, they lead to at least a temporary relief from the tyranny of reason and from the pressure of the external world. In *A Midsummer Night's Dream* the dominance of the Lord of Misrule is not marked by coarse parody, but by the partial repeal of the laws of cause and effect. By delicate beauty, gentle mockery, and simple romantic foolishness our freedom is gained.

If Shakespeare's play had, like *Comus*, been based upon an abstract idea, he might have found in Malvolio, not in Bottom, the most effective contrast to the Fairy Queen. The contrast between the prosaic man of business and the pierrot or elfin type of creature is a recurrent theme in literature. The amusement lies in putting the prosy people in charming or unconventional surroundings and laughing at their inadequacy and confusion—

> Big fat woman whom nobody loves,
> Why do you walk through the fields with gloves,
> Missing so much and so much?

But either gloves or yellow stockings and cross garters would shatter Shakespeare's dream. For his play is not a criticism of life but a dance, and a dance of which the underlying motif is harmony. The contrast may be sharp as you please, but the unity must be deeper than the divergence. For, after all, the presiding deity is Hymen. His functions are performed by the fairies who are, indeed, emanations from him. Deeply rooted in folklore is the connection between the fairies and fertility, and Shakespeare had a happy inspiration when he substituted them for the Ceres, Dianas, and Junos of pageantry, and also turned them into an expression of the harmony and concord which was the keystone of most Elizabethan revels.

* * *

MURIEL C. BRADBROOK (1909–   )

Muriel C. Bradbrook is a reader in England at Cambridge University, since 1932 a Fellow of Girton College, Cambridge, and since 1962 Vice Mistress of Girton. In 1958–1959 she was a visiting scholar at the Folger Library in Washington and at the Henry E. Huntington Library at Pasadena, California. From the beginning of her career to the present, she has written with authority and charm on the Elizabethan stage and the dramas designed for it. The following are some of her best-known volumes: *Elizabethan Stage Conditions* (1932), *Themes· and Conventions of Elizabethan Tragedy* (1934), *Shakespeare and Elizabethan Poetry* (1951), *The Growth and Structure of Elizabethan Comedy* (1955), and *The Rise of the Common Player* (1962).

Miss Bradbrook analyzes the plot of *A Midsummer Night's Dream* from the point of view of its structure. It is built on a series of contrasts—three contrasted worlds, the lovers, the rustics, and the fairies, and the plot is in contrast with the subplot.

THE IMPORTANCE OF CONTRAST IN THE STRUCTURE OF
A Midsummer Night's Dream
(from: *Shakespeare and Elizabethan Poetry*, 1951)

In *A Midsummer Night's Dream* Shakespeare did not rely either on old stories or old plays. There may be faint traces of Chaucer, but the whole thing is virtually his own. Three contrasted worlds—the lovers', the rustics', and the fairies'—

have each their own idiom and their own codes, but in the woods of Athens, as in the Forest of Arden, divided worlds meet and intermingle. This simple trick of contrasted plot and subplot has in it the germ of all Shakespeare's later construction—it shows the artist's eye that could pick out an old chronicle play, crude but serviceable, and a story from the most elegant fiction of the day, put them together and make *King Lear*. His mind full of images of the countryside, and Ovid's *Metamorphoses* (for he had not long since written *Venus and Adonis*, where the two combined), the distressed lovers who were parted by their family, and a picture of Queen Mab (for he had also not long since written *Romeo and Juliet*) Shakespeare combined them, perhaps for a wedding masque, and wrote *A Midsummer Night's Dream*.

The lovers of the Athenian Court are drawn in a spirit of parody perfectly in keeping with an occasion which would mark the triumphant end of a real courtship. They are, moreover, contrasted with the heroic loves of Theseus and Hippolita.

The opening scene, daylight and Athens, maintains a formal style which sets the death penalty hanging over Hermia and the treachery of Helena in their proper perspective. The bouts of wit between Hermia and Lysander or Hermia and Helena are on professedly serious subjects, but their manner is that of Valentine's exchanges with Thurio:

Hermia. I frowne upon him, yet he loues me still
Helena. O that your frownes would teach my smiles such skil . . .
Hermia. The more I hate, the more he followes mee
Helena. The more I loue, the more he hateth mee
Hermia. His folly, *Helena*, is no fault of mine.

Helena. None but your beauty; would that fault were mine.

(1.i. 194–201)

Yet here and there, within the scene, there is heard an impersonal note of description, depicting love in terms of the natural world, which brings into the rhetorical stiffness of the dramatic exchanges such lively contrasts as that of the holy maids 'chanting faint hymnes to the cold fruitless Moone', and the sound of Hermia's voice:

> More tuneable then Larke, to shepherdes eare,
> When wheat is greene, when hauthorne buddes appeare.

(1. i. 184–5)

So after Egeus's speech—quite in the tone of Old Capulet—on Lysander's wicked use of love tokens, songs at the window by moonlight, and other means 'of strong prevailment in unhardened youth' there is a more powerful echo of the loves of *Romeo and Juliet*.

> If there were a sympathy in choice,
> Warre, death or sicknesse did lay siege to it,
> Making it momentany, as a sound:
> Swift as a shadow short as any dreame,
> Briefe as the lightning in the collied night,
> That (in a spleene) unfolds both heauen and earth,
> And ere a man hath power to say, behold,
> The iawes of darknesse do devour it up,
> So quicke bright thinges come to confusion.

(1. i. 141–9)

Yet, taken in a different key, this confusion of darkness, swift brevity of love, and dangerous portents of the collied night are to be the lot of the quartet of lovers in their woodland wanderings. The enchantments of the night were a topic of the hour: Nashe had recently written a not altogether serious pamphlet on them, in a tone of rustic credulity.

The nocturnal was itself a recognized species at a later date, with 'the mistakes of a night' providing the opportunity for broad farce. The *Two Angry Women of Abingdon* is the best-known example where the wrangling of the good wives and the runaway antics of Moll and Frank weave a homespun version of some of Shakespeare's scenes. Shakespeare's only models were the fairy plays of Greene and Peele, *James IV*, *Friar Bacon*, and *The Old Wives' Tale*, all charming, innocent, and completely shapeless, depending upon the inconsequence of the folk tale and the 'shows' with which the early stage abounded. *A Midsummer Night's Dream* combines in the most paradoxical way the natural and to Elizabethan eyes pastoral and humble beauty of the woodland and its fairies with the highly sophisticated pattern of the lovers' quarrel and the straight burlesque provided by the loves of Pyramus and Thisbe. Seen from the courtly point of view, the play has many elements of the masque, as Miss Welsford pointed out: '*A Midsummer Night's Dream* is a dance, a movement of bodies. The plot is a pattern, a figure, rather than a series of events occasioned by human characters and passions, and this pattern, especially in the moonlight parts of the play, is the pattern of a dance.' The enchantments of Puck are a deft parody of the normal operation of fancy, which is

> engenderd in the eyes,
> With gazing fed,

and little more reasonable than his magic. Theseus describes the lover's power of metamorphosis:

> Louers and madmen haue such seething braines,
> Such shaping phantasies, that apprehend more
> Then coole reason euer comprehends . . .
> Sees *Helen's* beauty in a browe of *Egipt*.
>
> (v. i. 4–11)

This is a theme which was to be more subtly and fully explored in later plays, but the jests of Puck are not much beyond the ordinary scope of Cupid.

Bottom and his friends are drawn, as Mr. Sidgwick observed, 'from observation', but also from the stage clowns who have already been allowed to mock Valentine and Proteus. Their mimic play apes the flight from Athens, though of course the parallel is not visible either to them or to their highly condescending auditory: it is part of the 'mirror' technique of the play-within-the-play, where Bottom so laboriously makes everyone comfortable with explanations of the difference between life and art, and where the fun puts both players and audience together inside the jest of professional actors pretending to be mechanicals trying to be amateur actors before an unreal audience. There is a special pleasure in this play within the play from the actors' point of view, and the hilarious bit of business which is preserved by a contemporary reference, 'Like Thisbe in the play h'as almost killed himself with the scabbard', shows that it was played with gusto.

The mechanicals are out of their element when they get into the wood but the heroical Bottom is ready to adapt himself to any situation. His transformation may recall the tricks of witches, who sometimes loved and were loved by transformed animals: it may recall the *Golden Asse:* it may be mockery of the legend of Circe which held a tragical implication for Elizabethans: but it is primarily a comic Metamorphosis, a simple and splendid opportunity for the low comedian to bring off a telling stage hit. When Falstaff is transformed into a horned beast under the magic oak of Windsor Forest, the fairies might plead their most moral intentions, as they pinch him black and blue:

Fie on sinneful Phantasie: Fie on Lust and Luxurie:
Lust is but a bloody fire, kindled with unchaste desire. . . .

but the fairies of Athens have no such highmindedness.

Oberon, Titania, and Puck, though they were figures of folk-lore, are completely transformed in Shakespeare's imagination. (Greene's Oberon is a wizard who acts as Presenter to *James IV*.) It was he who devised the tiny fairy of modern fantasy, and his charming inventions were seized upon by his contemporaries almost at once. Drayton's *Nimphidia*, Herrick's *Oberon's Palace*, *Oberon's Feast*, and *Oberon's Chapel*, and the fairies of the Jacobean masques, derive from Shakespeare. In all his supernatural creations, he seems to have created completely new species of creatures, and these of all his characters were most eagerly copied by his contemporaries and immediate successors. The Witches in *Macbeth* were not the first attempt to present a serious treatment of the evil supernatural on the Elizabethan stage, but they set a fashion for witch plays; the spirits of *The Tempest* again set a fashion: Caliban is the prototype of the Witch's Son, a popular stage figure in Caroline drama, and Ariel made a deep impression on the Restoration stage. Throughout the seventeenth century Shakespeare's spirits and fairies served and inspired other playwrights and poets of all kinds.

The fairies are spirits of the woods and the flowers—their names betray them. The description of their life is a description of the woodland itself, its freckled cowslips, its wild thyme, oxlips, and nodding violets, its luscious woodbine. Titania woos Bottom in the accents of Drayton's Phoebe wooing his Endimion, even promising to transform him to a spirit, 'purged from earthly grossness'.

Her little fairies who attend on him and offer him their courtesies are exquisitely set off by his earthly if laboured politeness. The contrast is even bolder than that which put the description of Queen Mab into the mouth of the gracelessly broadspoken Mercutio: and perhaps in this clumsy response to the queenly proffer of love, the author of *Venus and Adonis* is providing a 'squandering glance' at his own earlier and somewhat fleshly idyll. Some light parody of *Romeo and Juliet* is also discernible. The fairies are born of that same minute observation which depicted the hunting of poor Wat, dew-bedabbled and scratched with briars, the snail:

> whose tender hornes being hit,
> Shrinks backward in his shellie cave with paine,

and from the chidden hounds of Adonis's hunt come the hounds of Theseus.

The whole anthropomorphic world of the Ovidian romance, the world of Lodge's *Scilla* and of Drayton's *Endimion and Phoebe*, is embodied in the magnificent speech of Titania which places the fairies in control of the whole natural scene, and evokes so richly and powerfully Nature's waste fertility, all to disorder wandering. This speech may be reminiscent of Vergil in his pastoral poetry; Titania's later appeal to Bottom recalls the Eclogues quite directly.

. . . .

In their recriminations over Theseus and Hippolita, Titania and her Oberon seem to be deputizing for the ancient gods, for Juno and Jove himself, so that their final appearance to bless and hallow the marriage bed is not unfitting for a king's bridal. They are masquers like the Masquers of Prospero's Vision, but the Masque is that of the whole flowery natural world—*Natura naturans*—blossoming, ripening, decaying and renewing. In spite of the fact that the picture in Titania's first speech is one of disorder, the effect is not destructive, or horrifying, or at all akin to the tragic speeches of *Richard II*, for example, which is of the same date as the *Dream*. If Titania's speech be compared with the gardeners' scene, it becomes clear that the natural beauties of the Queen's territory are not being used as symbols, or reflections in another mode, of the fairy quarrel, as she asserts they are; but rather that in the fairies themselves, as in those later 'elues of hils, brooks, standing lakes and groves' which Prospero invokes, the very quality of the too-much-loved earth has been given a local habitation and a name. Here if anywhere is the 'cause' and germ of the play:

> Neuer since the middle Summers spring
> Met we on hil, in dale, forest, or mead,
> By paved fountain or by rushie brooke

> Or in the beached margent of the sea,
> To dance our ringlets to the whistling winde. . . .
> The Spring, the Sommer
> The childing Autumn, angry Winter change
> Their wonted Liueries, and the mazed worlde
> By their increase, now knowes not which is which. . . .
>
> (II. i. 52 ff.)

The voice of Venus Genetrix is the same in Vergil's Sicily, or Shakespeare's England; the particular countryside, heavily wooded, with rushy streams, broad water meadows, and rich undulating pasture, is that of Warwick. As a faint light beside the full splendour of Shakespeare's play may be set Nashe's *Summers Last Will and Testament*, with its figures of Winter and Back-Winter, its song of

> Spring the sweet spring is the years pleasant king

alternating with the grim picture of the plague-stricken city from which the entertainers have fled to the safety of Croydon. But compared with Shakespeare, this is an artless piece of revelry. His first completely individual comedy was to remain, *sui generis*, a 'species' of which only one specimen was found in nature.

*　　*　　*

C. L. BARBER (1913–　　)

Professor C. L. Barber began his academic career as a Junior Fellow of the Society of Fellows at Harvard University. Later he served for two years as a Fellow at the Folger Shakespeare Library at Washington. He was first a Professor of English at Amherst College and now holds a similar post at the University of Indiana.

In the following excerpt, Barber shows that May Day games provided Shakespeare with a pattern for all the features of *A Midsummer Night's Dream*. On May Day young people, on pleasure bent, went to the woods and meadows of the countryside to perform their rites to the day. However, Shakespeare did not expect his audiences to think that the action was taking place on the actual May Day as fixed by the calendar. Youth and maidens went Maying at various times of the year, so that the Maying of the play could be thought of as happening on Midsummer Eve (June 23).

THE RELATION OF *A Midsummer Night's Dream* TO MAY DAY GAMES
(from: *Shakespeare's Festive Comedy*, 1959)

If Shakespeare had called *A Midsummer Night's Dream* by a title that referred to pageantry and May games, the aspects of it with which I shall be chiefly concerned would be more often discussed. To honor a noble wedding, Shakespeare gathered up in a play the sort of pageantry which was usually presented piece-meal at aristocratic entertainments, in park and court as well as in hall. And the May game, everybody's pastime, gave the pattern for his whole action, which moves "from the town to the grove" and back again, bringing in summer to the bridal. These things were familiar and did not need to be stressed by a title.

Shakespeare's young men and maids, like those Stubbes described in May games, "run gadding over night to the woods, . . . where they spend the whole night in pleasant pastimes—" and in the fierce vexation which often goes with the pastimes of falling in and out of love and threatening to fight about it. "And no marvel," Stubbes exclaimed about such headlong business, "for there is a great Lord present among them, as superintendent and Lord over their pastimes and sports, namely, Satan, prince of hell." In making Oberon, prince of fairies, into the May king, Shakespeare urbanely plays with the notion of a supernatural power at work in holiday: he presents the common May game presided over by an aristocratic garden god. Titania is a Summer Lady who "waxeth wounder proud":

> I am a spirit of no common rate,
> The summer still doth tend upon my state . . .
> (III.i.157–158)

And Puck, as jester, promotes the "night-rule" version of misrule over which Oberon is superintendent and lord in the "haunted grove." The lovers originally meet

> in the wood, a league without the town,
> Where I did meet thee once with Helena
> To do observance to a morn of May.
> (I.i.165–167)

Next morning, when Theseus and Hippolyta find the lovers sleeping, it is after their own early "observation is performed"

—presumably some May-game observance, of a suitably aristocratic kind, for Theseus jumps to the conclusion that

> No doubt they rose up early to observe
> The rite of May; and, hearing our intent,
> Came here in grace of our solemnity.
> (IV.i.135–137)

These lines need not mean that the play's action happens on May Day. Shakespeare does not make himself accountable for exact chronological inferences; the moon that will be new according to Hippolyta will shine according to Bottom's almanac. And in any case, people went Maying at various times, "Against May, Whitsunday, and other time" is the way Stubbes puts it. This Maying can be thought of as happening on a midsummer night, even on Midsummer Eve itself, so that its accidents are complicated by the delusions of a magic time. (May Week at Cambridge University still comes in June.) The point of the allusions is not the date, but the *kind* of holiday occasion. The Maying is completed when Oberon and Titania with their trains come into the great chamber to bring the blessings of fertility. They are at once common and special, a May king and queen making their good luck visit to the manor house, and a pair of country gods, half-English and half-Ovid, come to bring their powers in tribute to great lords and ladies.

The play's relationship to pageantry is most prominent in the scene where the fairies are introduced by our seeing their quarrel. This encounter is the sort of thing that Elizabeth and the wedding party might have happened on while walking about in the park during the long summer dusk. The fairy couple accuse each other of the usual weakness of pageant personages—a compelling love for royal personages:

> Why art thou here,
> Come from the farthest steep of India,
> But that, forsooth, the bouncing Amazon,
> Your buskin'd mistress and your warrior love,
> To Theseus must be wedded, and you come
> To give their bed joy and prosperity?
>
> (II.i.68–73)

Oberon describes an earlier entertainment, very likely one in which the family of the real-life bride or groom had been concerned:

> My gentle Puck, come hither. Thou rememb'rest
> Since once I sat upon a promontory
> And heard a mermaid, on a dolphin's back . . .
> That very time I saw (but thou couldst not)
> Flying between the cold moon and the earth
> Cupid, all arm'd. A certain aim he took
> At a fair Vestal, throned by the West,
> And loos'd his love-shaft smartly from his bow,
> As it should pierce a hundred thousand hearts.
> But I might see young Cupid's fiery shaft
> Quench'd in the chaste beams of the wat'ry moon,
> And the imperial vot'ress passed on,
> In maiden meditation, fancy-free.
>
> (II.i.147–164)

At the entertainment at Elvetham in 1591, Elizabeth was throned by the west side of a garden lake to listen to music from the water; the fairy queen came with a round of dancers and spoke of herself as wife of Auberon. These and other similarities make it quite possible, but not necessary, that Shakespeare was referring to the Elvetham occasion. There has been speculation, from Warburton on down, aimed at identifying the mermaid and discovering in Cupid's fiery shaft a particular bid for Elizabeth's affections; Leicester's Kenilworth entertainment in 1575 was usually taken as the occasion alluded to, despite the twenty years that had gone by when Shakespeare wrote. No one, however, has cogently demonstrated any reference to court intrigue—which is to be expected in view of the fact that the play, after its original performance, was on the public stage. The same need for discretion probably accounts for the lack of internal evidence as to the particular marriage the comedy originally celebrated. But what is not in doubt, and what matters for our purpose here, is the *kind* of occasion Oberon's speech refers to, the kind of occasion Shakespeare's scene is shaped by. The speech describes, in retrospect, just such a joyous overflow of pleasure into music and make-believe as is happening in Shakespeare's own play. The fact that what Shakespeare handled with supreme skill was just what was most commonplace no doubt contributes to our inability to connect what he produced with particular historical circumstances.

As we have seen, it was commonplace to imitate Ovid. Ovidian fancies pervade *A Midsummer Night's Dream*, and especially the scene of the fairy quarrel: the description of the way Cupid "loos'd his love shaft" at Elizabeth parallels the Metamorphoses' account of the god's shooting "his best arrow, with the golden head" at Apollo; Helena, later in the scene, exclaims that "The story shall be chang'd:/ Apollo flies, and Daphne holds the chase"—and proceeds to invert animal images from Ovid. The game was not so much to lift things gracefully from Ovid as it was to make up fresh things in Ovid's manner, as Shakespeare here, by playful mythopoesis, explains the bad weather by his fairies' quarrel and makes up a metamorphosis of the little Western flower to motivate the play's follies and place Elizabeth superbly above them. The pervasive Ovidian influence accounts for Theseus' putting fables and fairies in the same breath when he says, punning on ancient and antic,

> I never may believe
> These antique fables nor these fairy toys.
> (V.i.2–3)

The humor of the play relates superstition, magic and passionate delusion as "fancy's images." The acutal title emphasizes a sceptical attitude by calling the comedy a "dream." It seems unlikely that the title's characterization of the dream, "a midsummer night's dream," implies association with the specific customs of Midsummer Eve, the shortest night of the year, except as "midsummer night" would carry suggestions of a magic time. The observance of Midsummer Eve in England centered on building bonfires or "bonefires," of which there is nothing in Shakespeare's moonlight play. It was a time when maids might find out who their true love would be by dreams or divinations. There were customs of decking houses with greenery and hanging lights, which just possibly might connect with the fairies' torches at the comedy's end. And when people gathered fern seed at midnight, sometimes they spoke of spirits whizzing invisibly past. If one ranges through the eclectic pages of *The Golden Bough*, guided by the index for Midsummer Eve, one finds other customs suggestive of Shakespeare's play, involving moonlight, seeing the moon in water, gathering dew, and so on, but in Sweden, Bavaria, or still more remote places, rather than England. One can assume that parallel English customs have been lost, or one can assume that Shakespeare's imagination found its way to similarities with folk cult, starting from the custom of Maying and the general feeling that spirits may be abroad in the long dusks and short nights of midsummer. Olivia in *Twelfth Night* speaks of "midsummer madness" (III.iv.61). In the absence of evidence, there is no way to settle just how much comes from tradition. But what *is* clear is that Shakespeare was not *simply* writing out folklore which he heard in his youth, as Romantic critics liked to assume. On the contrary, his fairies are produced by a complex fusion of pageantry and popular game, as well as popular fancy. Moreover, as we shall see, they are not serious in the menacing way in which the people's fairies were serious. Instead they are serious in a very different way, as embodiments of the May-game experience of eros in men and women and trees and flowers, while any superstitious tendency to believe in their literal reality is mocked. The whole night's action is presented as a release of shaping fantasy which brings clarification about the tricks of strong imagination. We watch a dream; but we are awake, thanks to pervasive humor about the tendency to take fantasy literally, whether in love, in superstition, or in Bottom's mechanical dramatics. As in *Love's Labour's Lost* the folly of wit becomes the generalized comic subject in the course of an astonishing release of witty invention, so here in the course of a more inclusive release of imagination, the folly of fantasy becomes the general subject, echoed back and forth between the strains of the play's imitative counterpoint.

. . . .

Moonlight and Moonshine: The Ironic Burlesque .

The consciousness of the creative or poetic act itself, which pervades the main action, explains the subject-matter of the burlesque accompaniment provided by the clowns. If Shakespeare were chiefly concerned with the nature of love, the clowns would be in love, after their fashion. But instead, they are putting on a play. That some commoners should honor the wedding, in their own way, along with the figures from pageantry, is of course in keeping with the purpose of gathering into a play the several sorts of entertainments usually presented separately. But an organic purpose is served too: the clowns provide a broad burlesque of the mimetic impulse to become something by acting it, the impulse which in the main action is fulfilled by imagination and understood by humor. Bottom feels he can be anything: "What is Pyramus, a lover, or a tyrant? . . . An I may hide my face, let me play Thisby too . . . Let me play the lion too." His soul would like to fly out into them all; but he is *not* Puck! In dealing with dramatic illusion, he and the other mechanicals are invincibly literal-minded, carrying to absurdity the tendency to treat the imaginary as though it were real. They exhibit just the all-or-nothing attitude towards fancy which would be fatal to the play as a whole.

When the clowns think that Bottom's transformation has

deprived them of their chief actor, their lament seems pointedly allusive to Shakespeare's company and their play.

> *Snug.* Masters, the Duke is coming from the temple, and there is two or three lords and ladies more married. If our sport had gone forward, we had all been made men.
> *Flute.* O sweet bully Bottom! Thus hath he lost sixpence a day during his life. He could not have scaped sixpence a day. An the Duke had not given him sixpence a day for playing Pyramus, I'll be hanged! He would have deserved it. Sixpence a day in Pyramus, or nothing!
>
> (IV.ii.15–24)

The repetition of "sixpence a day" seems loaded: if Bottom in Pyramus is worth sixpence, what is Kempe in Bottom worth? For Bottom is to Theseus as Kempe was to the nobleman for whom the play was first produced. The business about moonshine brings this out:

> *Quince.* . . . But there is two hard things: that is, to bring the moonlight into a chamber; for, you know, Pyramus and Thisby meet by moonlight.
> *Snout.* Doth the moon shine that night we play our play?
> *Bottom.* A calendar, a calendar! Look in the almanac. Find out moonshine, find out moonshine!
> *Quince.* Yes, it doth shine that night.
> *Bottom.* Why, then may you leave a casement of the great chamber window, where we play, open, and the moon may shine in at the casement.
> *Quince.* Ay; or else one must come in with a bush of thorns and a lantern, and say he comes to disfigure, or to present, the person of Moonshine.
>
> (III.i.47–63)

Shakespeare, in *his* play, triumphantly accomplishes just this hard thing, "to bring the moonlight into a chamber." The moonshine, here and later, shows how aware Shakespeare was of what his plastic imagination was doing with moonlight. Since the great chamber Bottom speaks of was, at the initial private performance, the very chamber in which the Chamberlain's men were playing, "Pyramus and Thisby" adorns Theseus' fictitious wedding just as *A Midsummer Night's Dream* adorns the real wedding. Bottom's proposal to open a casement reduces the desire for realism to the absurdity of producing the genuine article. Translated out of irony, it suggests, that "if you want real moonlight, you put yourself in Bottom's class." It is amusing how later producers have labored with ever greater technical resources to achieve Bottom's ideal. Hollywood's Max Reinhardt version omitted most of the poetry to make room for cellophane-spangled fairies standing in rows on ninety-foot moonbeams.

The difference between art and life is also what the clowns forget in their parlous fear lest "the ladies be afeared of the lion" and the killing. Bottom's solution is to tell the ladies in plain language that fiction is not fact:

Write me a prologue; and let the prologue seem to say, we will do no harm with our swords, and that Pyramus is not kill'd indeed; and for the more better assurance, tell them that I Pyramus am not Pyramus, but Bottom the weaver. This will put them out of fear.

(III.i.18–23)

Now this expresses Bottom's vanity, too. But producers and actors, bent on showing "character," can lose the structural, ironic point if they let the lines get lost in Bottom's strutting. What the clowns forget, having "never labour'd in their minds till now," is that a killing or a lion in a play, however plausibly presented, is a mental event. Because, like children, they do not discriminate between imaginary and real events, they are literal about fiction. But they are not *un*imaginative: on the contrary they embody the stage of mental development before the discipline of facts has curbed the tendency to equate what is "in" the mind with what is "outside" it. They apply to drama the same sort of mentality that supports superstition—it is in keeping that the frightening sort of folk beliefs about changelings are for them an accepted part of life: "Out of doubt he is transported." Because this uncritical imaginativeness is the protoplasm from which all art develops, the clowns are as delightful and stimulating as they are ridiculous. Even while we are laughing at them, we recover sympathetically the power of fantasy enjoyed by children, who, like Bottom, can be anything, a train, an Indian or a lion.

In the performance of *Pyramus and Thisby*, Shakespeare captures the naïveté of folk dramatics and makes it serve his controlling purpose as a final variant of imaginative aberration. The story from Ovid, appropriate for a burlesque in an Ovidian play, is scarcely the kind of thing the simple people would have presented in life; but their method and spirit in putting it on, and the spirit in which the noble company take it, are not unlike what is suggested by Laneham's account of the bride-ale show at Kenilworth. "If we imagine no worse of them than they of themselves," Theseus observes of the Athenian artisans, "they may pass for excellent men" (V.i.218). The comedy of the piece centers not so much on what is acted in it as in the continual failure to translate actor into character. Shakespeare's skill is devoted to keeping both the players and their would-be play before us at the same time, so that we watch, not Pyramus alone, nor Bottom alone, but Bottom "in Pyramus," the fact of the one doing violence to the fiction of the other.

Almost half of *Pyramus and Thisby* is taken up with prologues of the sort one gets in the mummers' plays:

> I am king of England,
> As you may plainly see.

Such prologues suit Shakespeare's purpose, because they present the performer openly climbing in the window of aesthetic illusion, where he can get stuck midway:

> In this same enterlude it doth befall
> That I, one Snout by name, present a wall . . .
> This loam, this roughcast, and this stone doth show
> That I am that same wall. The truth is so.
>
> (V.i.156–163)

"The truth is so," by warranting that fiction is fact, asks for a laugh, as does the Prologue's "At the which let no man wonder," or Moon's

> Myself the man i' the moon *do seem to be.*

The incarnation of Wall is a particularly "happy-unhappy" inspiration, because the more Wall does, the less he is a wall and the more he is Snout.

There is a great deal of incidental amusement in the parody and burlesque with which *Pyramus and Thisby* is loaded. It burlesques the substance of the death scene in *Romeo and Juliet* in a style which combines ineptitudes from Golding's translation of Ovid with locutions from the crudest doggerel drama. What is most remarkable about it, however, is the way it fits hilarious fun into the whole comedy's development of attitude and understanding. After the exigent poise of the humorous fantasy, laughs now explode one after another; and yet they are still on the subject, even though now we are romping reassuringly through easy-to-make distinctions. Theseus can say blandly

The best in this kind are but shadows; and the worst are no worse, if imagination amend them.   (V.i.214–216)

Although we need not agree (Hippolyta says "It must be your imagination then, and not theirs."), Theseus expresses part of our response—a growing detachment towards imagination, moving towards the distance from the dream expressed in Puck's epilogue.

The meeting in the woods of Bottom and Titania is the climax of the polyphonic interplay; it comes in the middle of the dream, when the humor has the most work to do. Bottom in the ass's head provides a literal metamorphosis, and in the process brings in the element of grotesque fantasy which the Savage Man or Woodwose furnished at Kenilworth, a comic version of an animal-headed dancer or of the sort of figure Shakespeare used in Herne the Hunter, "with great ragged horns," at the oak in *The Merry Wives of Windsor*. At the same time he is the theatrical company's clown "thrust in my head and shoulder to play a part in majestical matters" and remaining uproariously literal and antipoetic as he does so. Titania and he are fancy against fact, not beauty and the beast. She makes all the advances while he remains very respectful, desiring nothing bestial but "a peck of provender." Clownish oblivion to languishing beauty is sure-fire comedy on any vaudeville stage. Here it is elaborated in such a way that when Titania is frustrated, so is the transforming power of poetry:

> *Titania.* I pray thee, gentle mortal, sing again.
> Mine ear is much enamoured of thy note;
> So is mine eye enthralled to thy shape;
> And thy fair virtue's force (perforce) doth move me,
> On the first view, to say, to swear, I love thee.
> *Bottom.* Methinks, mistress, you should have little reason for that. And yet, to say the truth, reason and love keep little company together now-a-days. The more the pity that some honest neighbours will not make them friends. Nay, I can gleek, upon occasion.
> *Titania.* Thou art as wise as thou art beautiful.
> *Bottom.* Not so, neither . . .
>
> (III.i.140–152)

From a vantage below romance, the clown makes the same point as sceptical Theseus, that reason and love do not go together. Titania tells him that she

> . . . will purge thy mortal grossness so
> That thou shalt like an airy spirit go.
>
> (III.i.163–164)

But even her magic cannot "transpose" Bottom.

The "low" or "realistic" effect which he produces when juxtaposed with her is much less a matter of accurate imitation of common life than one assumes at first glance. Of course the homely touches are telling—forms of address like "Methinks, mistress" or words like *gleek* suggest a social world remote from the elegant queen's. But the realistic effect does not depend on Bottom's being like real weavers, but on the *détente* of imaginative tension, on a downward movement which counters imaginative lift. This antipoetic action involves, like the poetic, a high degree of abstraction from real life, including the control of rhythm which can establish a blank verse movement in as little as a single line, "Thou art as wise as thou art beautiful," and so be able to break the ardent progression of the queen's speech with "Not so, neither." When Bottom encounters the fairy attendants, he reduces the fiction of their existence to fact:

> *Bottom.* I cry your worships mercy, heartily. I beseech your worship's name.
> *Cobweb.* Cobweb.
> *Bottom.* I shall desire you of more acquaintance, good Master Cobweb. If I cut my finger, I shall make bold with you.
>
> (III.i.182–187)

Cobwebs served the Elizabethans for adhesive plaster, so that when Bottom proposes to "make bold with" Cobweb, he treats him as a *thing*, undoing the personification on which the little fellow's life depends. To take hold of Cobweb in this way is of course a witty thing to do, when one thinks about it. But since the wit is in the service of a literal tendency, we can take it as the expression of a "hempen homespun." There is usually a similar incongruity between the "stupidity" of a clown and the imagination and wit required to express such stupidity. Bottom's charming combination of ignorant exuberance and oblivious imaginativeness make him the most humanly credible and appealing personality Shakespeare had yet created from the incongruous qualities required for the clown's role. The only trouble with the part, in practice, is that performers become so preoccupied with bringing out the weaver's vanity as an actor that they lose track of what the role is expressing as part of the larger imaginative design.

For there is an impersonal, imaginative interaction between the clowning and the rest of the play which makes the clowns mean more than they themselves know and more than they are as personalities. Bottom serves to represent, in so aware a play, the limits of awareness, limits as limitations—and also, at moments, limits as form and so strength.

Bottom. Where are these lads? Where are these hearts?
Quince. Bottom! O most courageous day! O most happy hour!
Bottom. Masters, I am to discourse wonders; but ask me not what. For if I tell you, I am no true Athenian. I will tell you everything, right as it fell out.
Quince. Let us hear, sweet Bottom.
Bottom. Not a word of me. All that I will tell you is, that the Duke hath dined. Get your apparel together, good strings to your beards . . .

(IV.ii.26–36)

It is ludicrous for Bottom to be so utterly unable to cope with the "wonders," especially where he is shown boggling in astonishment as he wordlessly remembers them: "I have had a most rare vision. I have had a dream past the wit of man to say what dream it was" (IV.i.207–209). But there is something splendid, too, in the way he exuberantly rejoins "these lads" and takes up his particular, positive life as a "true Athenian." Metamorphosis cannot faze him for long. His imperviousness, indeed, is what is most delightful about him with Titania: he remains so completely himself, even in her arms, and despite the outward change of his head and ears; his confident, self-satisfied tone is a triumph of consistency, persistence, existence.

Notes

DATE: Although the date of the play cannot be determined with certainty, some topical allusions make 1594–1595 the probable year of its composition. The most helpful of these allusions is Titania's description of the abnormally rainy year of 1594 (Act II, Scene 1, lines 81–117). So wet and windy was the weather that it so completely changed the character of the seasons that no one could tell which was which. The comedy, therefore, must have been written in 1595 when everyone remembered the floods, the failure of the harvests, the consequent rise in prices, and the resultant financial distress. The year was also crucial for the Earl of Hertford's efforts to establish the legitimacy of his son, "the little changeling boy," and thus make him the rightful heir to the throne (see p. 7). Some critics find an allusion to the death of Robert Greene (1592) in the following lines of the play:

> The thrice three Muses mourning for the death
> Of Learning, late deceased in beggary.
> That is some satire, keen and critical

(Act V, Scene 1, lines 52–54.) The passing of Greene in wretched poverty made a strong impression on his fellow dramatists. The authors of many pamphlets appearing from 1592 to 1595 took the occasion as an opportunity for moral warning to the dissolute group of young University graduates who were establishing careers in the theatre.

TEXT: The only reliable text is that of the carelessly printed First Quarto. It appeared about two months after the play had been entered in the *Stationer's Register* to Thomas Fisher, on October 8, 1600. Its copy was a manuscript promptbook that may have been written in Shakespeare's own hand. The title of the First Quarto reads: "A Midsummer Night's Dream. As it hath beene sundry times publickely acted by the Right honourable, the Lord Chamberlaine his servants. Written by William Shakespeare." The Second Quarto (1619, fraudulently dated 1600) reprints the First Quarto; the First Folio Text is that of the Second Quarto. In the Quartos there are no divisions into acts and scenes. Acts but not scenes are marked in the First Folio.

SOURCE: The plot is Shakespeare's invention. Its various elements had different sources. The cross wooing and confusion of two pairs of lovers was a convention of Italian comedy, which Shakespeare had exploited in *The Two Gentlemen of Verona*. The main facts about Theseus and the Amazon Queen Hippolyta he found in Chaucer's *Knight's Tale*, where the poet refers to a great feast at their wedding. Shakespeare seems also to have read the Life of Theseus in Plutarch's *Lives*. For the tale of Pyramus and Thisbe, he had only to recall what he had read in Ovid's *Metamorphoses* at school. For the stories about fairies, Puck and Robin Goodfellow, he had no need for treatises. His head was crammed with folk-tales and nursery legends of elves, fairies, and hobgoblins which he had heard in his childhood. Midsummer Day was a widely celebrated holiday and Midsummer Night was the appointed hour for the roundup of all manner of witches and fairies.

CHARACTERS: THESEUS was a legendary king of Athens, whose exploits Shakespeare found in Plutarch. He defeated HIPPOLYTA, Queen of the Amazons, and married her. Thus he could say, "Hippolyta, I wooed thee with my sword" (Act 1, Scene 1, line 16).

The names Oberon and Titania were unknown to English folklore. Robert Greene (1560–1592) had brought OBERON on the stage in *James IV* (1591) as the king of the fairies. His name first appeared in the Old French *chanson de geste,* "Huon de Bordeaux" (c. 1230) in which he was a dwarf possessing magic powers. An English translation of this work by John Bouchier, Lord Berners (1467–1533) had a great vogue throughout sixteenth-century England.

PUCK—originally a Welsh name—is a sprite who does no greater harm than mischievously to lead wanderers astray. In English folklore he was often identified with Robin Goodfellow, a more earthy and domestic woodland sprite.

TITANIA—name Shakespeare found in Ovid.

QUINCE (or quoin)—the carpenter. A quoin is a wedge of wood. (The name of each artisan suggests his craft.)

FLUTE—the mender of the flutes or the pipes of an organ.

BOTTOM—the weaver. Bottom is the core of a ball of yarn and the ball itself.

SNOUT—the tinker. Snout is the nozzle of a kettle, the principal item a tinker would mend.

SNUG—the joiner, the maker of snug joints.

STARVELING—the tailor. A starveling is a starved, lean person, a description proverbially applied to tailors.

A NOTE ON SHAKESPEARE'S GRAMMAR: In Shakespeare's day the syntax and other aspects of English grammar and vocabulary were in a state of transition from an earlier, highly inflected language. The loss of endings obscured the distinguishing marks of various parts of speech, and the result was not so much confusion as freedom. (A full exposition of the peculiarities of Elizabethan language may be found in Abbott's *A Shakespearian Grammar*, 3d ed., 1871.)

This note will reassure the reader that constructions which seem ungrammatical were justified according to the accepted canons of Elizabethan usage.

VERSE: In *A Midsummer Night's Dream* Shakespeare employs prose for the dialogue of the artisans, rhymed verse for the dialogue of the fairies and the lovers when under fairy enchantment, and elsewhere blank verse. Shakespeare regularly employs rhymed verse for masques, and other plays within plays, to make the medium of this inserted drama distinct from the medium of other discourse.

*   *   *

ACT I, Scene 1

1. Lines 1–2
   Now, fair Hippolyta, our nuptial hour
   Draws on apace.
   The wedding of Theseus and Hippolyta was suggested by the lines at the beginning of Chaucer's *Knight's Tale:* "There wedded he the Queen, Hippolyta / And brought her home with him to his country."

2. Lines 30–2
Thou hast . . . stolen the impression of her fantasy. Thou hast captured her imagination by impressing your image upon it.

3. Lines 70–3
You can endure the livery of a nun,
For aye to be in shady cloister mewed,
To live a barren sister all your life,
Chanting faint hymns to the cold fruitless moon.
(See Note 4.)

4. Lines 89–90
Or on Diana's altar to protest
For aye austerity and single life.
Theseus refers first (Note 3) to the life of a Christian nun and then to a priestess in the service of Diana—the classical goddess of the moon and chastity.

Anachronisms are frequent in Shakespeare's work but the mixture of mediaeval monasticism and ancient mythology in the same connection within a few lines is an extreme example. In dream fantasy, however, such contradictions are of no importance.

5. Line 136
O cross! Too high to be enthralled to low. Oh misfortune! Too high in rank to be made the servant to one of low birth.

6. Lines 173–4
And by that fire which burned the Carthage queen,
When the false Troyan under sail was seen.
According to Virgil's *Aeneid* (Book IV) when Dido saw Aeneas sail away from Carthage toward Italy, she burned herself to death on a funeral pyre.

7. Line 182

Demetrius loves your fair. Fair stands for fairness and here means "blond beauty." It is evident throughout the play that Helena is a tall blonde and Hermia a short brunette.

8. Lines 209–10
Tomorrow night, when Phoebe doth behold
Her silver visage in the watery glass.
In classical mythology Phoebe was one of the names of the moon goddess.

9. Line 235
And therefore is winged Cupid painted blind. Cupid (Latin, "Desire"), the son of Venus, is the Roman equivalent of Eros, the Greek god of love. He is usually represented as a winged boy, equipped with bow and arrow and sometimes with his eyes covered with a bandage.

ACT I, SCENE 2
10. Line 2
You were best to call them generally. Bottom means "separately" or "severally." This is the first of his many malapropisms. For the rest of the play we have not identified any glosses as malapropisms.

11. Lines 30–2
I could play Ercles rarely, or a part to tear a cat in, to make all split. Ercles is a corrupt form of Heracles (Hercules), the classical hero. In early plays his speeches were filled with rant. "Tearing a cat" was proverbial for ranting. "Make all split" is akin to the milder, more modern "make the rafters ring."

12. Lines 37–8
And Phibbus' car
Shall shine from far.

In classical mythology Phoebus (Phibbus) was the sun god, who every day drove his chariot across the sky from east to west.

13. Lines 54–5
I'll speak in a monstrous little voice—"Thisne, Thisne." This mispronunciation has been thought to be part of the ridicule of the effeminate King James VI of Scotland, who lisped.

14. Line 114
hold or cut bow-strings. That is, be on hand or give up the play.

ACT II, Scene 1

15. Lines 8–9
And I serve the fairy queen,
To dew her orbs upon the green.
Her orbs are the so-called "fairy rings," circles of grass higher than the rest of the greensward.

16. Line 10
And cowslips tall her pensioners be. The Queen's Pensioners were a squad of tall, handsome gentlemen, magnificently costumed, who served as her bodyguard.

17. Line 23
She never had so sweet a changeling. A changeling is an infant left by the fairies to take the place of a baby they have stolen.

18. Lines 33–4
Or else you are that shrewd and knavish sprite
Called Robin Goodfellow.
In some scenes of the comedy, Shakespeare identifies Puck, the tiny court-jester of Oberon, the king of the fairies, with

Robin Goodfellow, a rural goblin, Milton's "lubber friend," who will enter the kitchen and do the housework by night, in return for a bowl of milk set out for him on the doorstep (see Note 70). The grotesque pranks that Puck describes (Act II, Scene 1, lines 43–57) are mischief of a cruder sort than anything that Puck actually does anywhere in this fantasy.

19. Lines 53–4
Then slip I from her bum, down topples she,
And "Tailor" cries, and falls into a cough.
The allusion to " 'Tailor' cries" is obscure. Kittredge suggests that after the old woman has fallen on the floor her position will be like that of a tailor at work squatting on the floor with his legs crossed.

20. Lines 66–8
And in the shape of Corin sat all day,
Playing on pipes of corn and versing love
To amorous Phillida.
"Corin" and "Phillida" were conventional names of shepherds in pastoral literature. Pipes of corn are pipes made out of oaten straws.

21. Lines 77–80
Didst thou not lead him through the glimmering night
From Perigenia, whom he ravished,
And make him with fair Aegle break his faith,
With Ariadne and Antiopa?
According to Plutarch, Perigenia, Aegle, Ariadne, and Antiopa were women whom Theseus loved.

22. Line 98
The nine men's morris is filled up with mud. Nine men's mor-

ris were squares on the village green marked out by nine stones on which the games were played.

23. Line 163
And the imperial votaress passed on. A votaress is a woman consecrated by a vow, in this case of chastity, the allusion being to Queen Elizabeth I.

24. Line 165
Yet marked I where the bolt of Cupid fell. The bolt of Cupid (see Note 9) was his arrow which awakened love when it pierced his victims.

25. Line 168
And maidens call it love-in-idleness. This innocent-sounding name for pansy meant to the Elizabethans "love-madness." There is a suggestion of this sense when Hamlet says (Act III, Scene 2, line 95), "They are coming to the play. I must be *idle*," that is, pretend to be mad for thwarted love; and when the Queen in the closet scene rebukes Hamlet (Act III, Scene 4, line 11): "Come, come, you answer with an *idle* tongue."

26. Lines 230–1
Run when you will, the story will be changed:
Apollo flies, and Daphne holds the chase.
In Ovid's *Metamorphoses* Apollo, the classical sun god (also known as Phoebus), followed the nymph Daphne, who was saved from him by being turned into a laurel tree.

27. Line 232
The dove pursues the griffin. The griffin, a fabulous creature with an eagle's head attached to the body of a lion, would, of course, do the pursuing of the dove.

ACT II, Scene 2

28. Lines 13–4
Philomel, with melody
Sing in our sweet lullaby.
Philomel is a poetic term for the nightingale based on Ovid's rendering of the classical Greek myth according to which Philomela, daughter of a king in ancient Greece, was turned into a nightingale.

ACT III, Scene 1

29. Lines 24–5
Well, we will have such a prologue; and it shall be written in eight and six. Eight and six are poems with alternate lines of eight and six syllables.

30. Lines 60–1
Ay; or else one must come in with a bush of thorns and a lanthorn. A folk tradition held that the Man in the Moon was a man who had been banished to the moon as punishment for gathering firewood on Sunday.

31. Line 97
Most brisky juvenal and eke most lovely Jew. The "Jew" is Flute's nonsensical repetition of the first syllable of "juvenal."

32. Line 99
I'll meet thee, Pyramus, at Ninny's tomb. Ninus was the hypothetical founder of Nineveh, the capital of the Assyrian Empire. In Ovid's story, the lovers, Pyramus and Thisbe, used to meet there.

33. Line 134
The plain-song cuckoo gray. In music "plainsong" was an ancient chant-melody of the church service. Bottom's punning reference means that the significance of "cuckoo" is clear, for

the sound resembles that of "cuckold," the husband of an unfaithful wife; and what married man dare contradict the bird's accusation?

ACT III, SCENE 2

34. Line 97
With sighs of love, that costs the fresh blood dear. This is an allusion to the belief that each sigh costs the heart a drop of blood.

35. Line 101
Swifter than arrow from the Tartar's bow. "Tartan" or "Tartar" was applied to soldiers of any of the invading Mongolian and Turkish hordes into eastern Europe from the thirteenth to the sixteenth centuries.

36. Line 141
That pure congealèd white, high Taurus' snow. Taurus is a mountain range in Asia Minor.

37. Lines 212–4
So, with two seeming bodies, but one heart;
Two of the first, like coats in heraldry,
Due but to one and crownèd with one crest.
The two bodies are like the double coat of arms in heraldry which belong to the husband and the wife, yet have only one crest—just as we have only one heart.

38. Line 329
of hindering knot-grass made. An infusion of knot-grass was supposed to stunt one's growth.

39. Line 357
as black as Acheron. In classical mythology Acheron is a river in Hades. The word has been used as a synonym for

Hades or Hell itself.

40. Line 379
For night's swift dragons cut the clouds full fast. Shakespeare conceived dragons as being yoked to the chariot which according to classical mythology Night drove across the heavens, between sunset and sunrise.

41. Line 380
And yonder shines Aurora's harbinger. In classical mythology, the goddess Aurora personified the dawn. The dawn's harbinger is the morning star.

42. Lines 382–3
>   *damned spirits all,*
> *That in crossways and floods have burial.*

Suicides were customarily buried, in unhallowed ground, at crossways (that is, crossroads). When the cause of death was drowning, their burial was in the sea. Their spirits were regarded as damned.

43. Line 388
But we are spirits of another sort. Not being infernal spirits, we are able to endure daylight.

44. Line 389
I with the morning's love have oft made sport. Morning's love is either Cephalus, a legendary Greek hunter who was loved by Aurora, the morning goddess, or possibly Aurora herself. Shakespeare found his story and that of his wife Procris in Ovid's *Metamorphoses* (see Note 60).

45. Line 392
Opening on Neptune with fair blessèd beams. Neptune is here identified with the sea, of which in classical mythology he was the god.

46. Line 463
The man shall have his mare again. This is a proverb meaning "Everything will be made right."

ACT IV, SCENE 1
47. Line 76
Dian's bud o'er Cupid's flower. Dian's bud was a plant, *Agnus castus*, which was thought to preserve chastity. (See Notes 3–4.)

48. Line 110
the music of my hounds. Elizabethan huntsmen chose hounds who bayed in harmony. (See also lines 127–8.)

49. Line 116
I was with Hercules and Cadmus once. In classical mythology Hercules (Greek Heracles) was a hero of miraculous strength and courage (see Note 11). Cadmus was a Phoenician youth who planted the teeth of a dragon he had slain, from which warriors sprang up who fought each other until only five survived. These five, led by Cadmus, founded Thebes.

50. Line 144
Begin these wood-birds but to couple now? Birds were supposed to choose their mates on St. Valentine's Day.

ACT V, SCENE 1
51. Line 8
Are of imagination all compact. Consist wholly of imagination.

52. Line 11
Sees Helen's beauty in a brow of Egypt. The lover sees in a dusky gypsy the beauty of Helen of Troy—regarded in the ancient world as the most beautiful of all women.

53. Lines 18–20

Such tricks hath strong imagination
That, if it would but apprehend some joy,
It comprehends some bringer of that joy.

Strong imagination can play such tricks that in apprehending a joy it conjures up some imaginary person as the bringer of the joy and includes him in it.

54. Line 44

The battle with the Centaurs. In Greek legend, a centaur had the head, trunk, and arms of a man but the body and legs of a horse. Ovid describes the defeat of the centaurs in a battle which arose at the wedding of Pirithous which Theseus attended.

55. Lines 48–9

The riot of the tipsy Bacchanals,
Tearing the Thracian singer in their rage.

The Thracian singer is Orpheus, the fabled musician, whose voice and lyre tamed even the wild beasts. Because of his rejection of all women in his inconsolable grief after the death of his wife Eurydice, he was torn limb from limb by frenzied maenads, female votaries of Bacchus, the classical god of wine.

56. Lines 52–3

The thrice three Muses mourning for the death
Of Learning, late deceased in beggary.

In classical mythology, the Muses were the nine goddesses who presided over song, the different kinds of poetry, and also the arts and sciences. The passage is often thought to refer to the death of Robert Greene who died in great misery in 1592.

57. Line 92

Takes it in might, not merit. About equivalent to "takes the will for the deed," or accepts the good intention of the performers.

58. Line 108

If we offend, it is with our good will. Quince perverts the sense of his speech by the blundering arrangement of his phrases.

59. Lines 117–9

THESEUS: *This fellow doth not stand upon points.*

LYSANDER: *He hath rid his prologue like a rough colt; he knows not the stop.* These lines contain two quibbles: "stands upon a point" means (1) "pays no attention to punctuation," (2) "does not care about trifles." "He knows not the stop" means (1) he knows not where to use a period and (2) he knows not how to signal his horse to stop.

60. Line 200

Not Shafalus to Procrus was so true. This is Bottom's blunder for Cephalus and Procris (see Note 44).

61. Lines 227–8

Then know that I, one Snug the joiner, am
A lion-fell, nor else no lion's dam.

Know that I am Snug the joiner and merely encased in the skin of a lion or a lioness. (Since "fell" also means fierce, an alternative interpretation—"I am neither a fierce lion nor lioness"—has been suggested.)

62. Line 244

He should have worn the horns on his head. This is the ancient joke about the horns which a cuckold, that is, a man whose wife was unfaithful, figuratively wore on his head.

63. Line 254

for, you see, it is already in snuff. A quibble on "in snuff," which meant (1) in need of snuffing, and (2) offended.

64. Line 289

Approach, ye Furies fell! The Furies (Erinyes) in classical mythology were the snaky-haired avenging spirits who pursued the guilty and inflicted madness. Their number, at first indefinite, was eventually three: Alecto, Megaera, and Tisiphone.

65. Line 290

O Fates, come, come. The Fates in classical mythology are the three goddesses supposed to determine the course of human life. They are Clotho, who spins the thread of human life; Lachesis, who determines its length; and Atropos, who cuts it off.

66. Line 291

Cut thread and thrum. The thrum is technically the fringelike end of the warp. The phrase means: cut the complete woven fabric of life.

67. Line 312

No die, but an ace. Demetrius is punning: (1) die for perish, and (2) die for the singular of dice.

68. Line 360

or to hear a Bergomask dance. This was a grotesque rustic dance named from the Italian town of Bergamo.

69. Line 391

By the triple Hecate's team. In classical mythology Hecate (usually pronounced Hek'at in Shakespeare) was a goddess combining the characters of moon goddess, earth goddess, and underworld goddess. In Greek art, the triple Hecate is represented with three heads and six arms.

70. Lines 396–7

I am sent with broom before,
To sweep the dust behind the door.

This is where Puck assumes some of the characteristics of Robin Goodfellow, a domestic sprite (see Note 18).

Bibliography

I. REFERENCE

BARTLETT, JOHN. *Concordance to Shakespeare*. London: The Macmillan Co., 1960. An invaluable reference book, containing a complete verbal index to words, phrases, and passages in all the plays and poems.

BROOKE, C. F. TUCKER. *Shakespeare of Stratford*. New Haven: Yale University Press, 1926. A handbook for students, gives the reader a brief, scholarly survey of the essential facts about the dramatist and his work.

COLLIER, J. P., and W. C. HAZLITT. *Shakespeare's Library: A Collection of the Romances, Novels, Poems, and Histories Used by Shakespeare in the Composition of His Works*. 2d ed. 6 vols. London: Reeves & Turner, 1875.

HALLIDAY, FRANK E. *A Shakespeare Companion 1564–1964*. New York: Schocken Books, 1964. An alphabetized list of critics, actors, plays, etc., and their relation to Shakespeare: an indispensable reference book.

HOLINSHED. *Shakespeare's Holinshed: The Chronicle and the Historical Plays*. Compared by W. G. Boswell-Stone. Rev. ed. London: Lawrence and Bullen, 1907.

———. *Holinshed's Chronicle as Used in Shakespeare's Plays*. Ed. Allardyce and Josephine Nicoll. New York: Everyman's Library, E. P. Dutton & Co., 1927.

INGLEBY, CLEMENT M. *Shakespeare's Century of Praise*. London: Trübner & Co., 1874. A history of opinion on Shakespeare and his work from 1591 to 1693. A source of information about the contemporary and early reputation of the Bard.

————. *Shakespeare Allusion Book: A Collection of Allusions to Shakespeare*. Rev., re-ed., rearranged. 2 vols. New York: Oxford University Press, 1932. These volumes bring the history of Shakespeare's reputation (first reported in *Shakespeare's Century of Praise*) down to the year 1932.

KÖKERITZ, HELGE. *Shakespeare's Pronunciation*. New Haven: Yale University Press, 1953. The latest authoritative work on this important subject.

KÖKERITZ, HELGE, and CHARLES TYLER PROUTY (eds.). *Shakespeare, William. Shakespeare's First Folio*. Facsimile ed. New Haven: Yale University Press, 1954. A photographic facsimile of the First Folio edition of Shakespeare's plays. An introduction on the printing of the Folio, playwriting, and the printing practices of Shakespeare's day prepared by Mr. Prouty.

SCHMIDT, ALEXANDER. *Shakespeare Lexicon*. 3d ed. 2 vols. Berlin: G. Reimer, 1902. The only complete dictionary of the English words, phrases, and constructions occurring in all the poet's works.

II. SHAKESPEARE'S LIFE

ALEXANDER, PETER. *Shakespeare's Life and Art*. London: James Nisbet & Co., 1939. Many important and new insights into the relation of Shakespeare's life to his art.

BRANDES, GEORG M. C. *William Shakespeare: A Critical Study*. Trans. William Archer. London: William Heinemann, 1902. A "life" by one of the most famous literary critics of the nineteenth century.

CHAMBERS, SIR EDMUND K. *William Shakespeare: A Study of Facts and Problems*. 2 vols. New York: Oxford University Press, 1930. A thorough assemblage of all the important facts of Shakespeare's life by the most rigorous scholar in the field.

CHUTE, MARCHETTE. *Shakespeare of London*. New York: E. P. Dutton & Co., 1949. An excellent biography of Shakespeare. It contains a bibliography.

DUTHIE, G. I. *Shakespeare*. London: Hutchinson, 1951. One of the best of modern biographies of Shakespeare, particularly interesting in the treatment of the comedies as presenting the antithesis between order and disorder.

FLEAY, F. G. *A Biographical Chronicle of the English Drama 1559–1642*. 2 vols. London: Reeves and Turner, 1891. One of the first surveys of the Elizabethan and Jacobean drama, by one of the leading members of the New Shakespeare Society, an originator of verse-tests to determine the authorship of plays.

LEE, SIR SIDNEY. *A Life of William Shakespeare*. 4th ed. New York: The Macmillan Co., 1929. For years the most authoritative account of the poet's life.

MUIR, K., and S. O'LOUGHLIN. *The Voyage to Illyria*. London: Methuen, 1937. A biography based on Shakespeare's sources and his imagery.

VAN DOREN, MARK. *Shakespeare*. New York: Doubleday and Co., 1953. An appreciation, particularly of the poetry in all Shakespeare's plays, by a sensitive critic, who is himself a poet.

III. SHAKESPEARE'S TIMES

GREY, W. W. *Henslowe's Diary*. 2 vols. London: H. H. Bullen, 1904–1908. The diary of Philip Henslowe covering the years 1592–1603. He gives the daily list of plays performed by the companies of which he was manager, and also his financial dealings with companies and actors. His records throw a flood of light on the many aspects of the Elizabethan stage.

JENKINS, ELIZABETH. *Elizabeth the Great*. New York: Coward-McCann, 1959. The most recent American biography, a distinguished piece of scholarship and literary skill.

MARDER, LOUIS. *His Exits and His Entrances, The Story of Shakespeare's Reputation*. Philadelphia: J. B. Lippincott, 1963. A newly published, useful book of reference.

NEALE, JOHN E. *Queen Elizabeth*. New York: Harcourt, Brace & Co., 1934. The authoritative biography.

RALEIGH, SIR WALTER. *Shakespeare's England: An Account of the Life and Manners of His Age*. 2 vols. Oxford: 1917. A complete account of the habits, interests, and activities of the people during Shakespeare's lifetime.

ROWSE, A. L. *The England of Elizabeth, The Structure of Society*. New York: The Macmillan Co., 1950.

STEEHOLM, CLARA and HARDY. *James I of England*. New York: Crown Publishers, 1938. A lively and acute account of James's personal life and kingship.

TILLYARD, E. M. W. *The Elizabethan World Picture*. New York: The Macmillan Co., 1944. The authoritative account of the geography—celestial and earthly—and the organization of the world as the Elizabethan pictured it.

IV. SHAKESPEARE'S THEATRE

ADAMS, JOHN C. *The Globe Playhouse: Its Design and Equipment*. Rev. ed. New York: Barnes and Noble, 1961. A widely approved description of the theatre for which most of Shakespeare's plays were written.

BALDWIN, T. W. *The Organization and Personnel of the Shake-

spearean Company. Princeton: Princeton University Press, 1927. Both a description of the organization of the company and an attempt to determine the roles of its principal actors, by one of the most learned of modern American scholars.

BECKERMAN, BERNARD. *Shakespeare at the Globe (1599–1609)*. New York: The Macmillan Co., 1962. An excellent recent study of all the elements of the production of Shakespeare's plays by his company at the Globe Theatre. By the Director of the Theatre at Hofstra College.

CHAMBERS, SIR EDMUND K. *The Elizabethan Stage*. 4 vols. Oxford: The Clarendon Press, 1923. The most complete account of the subject.

HARBAGE, ALFRED. *Shakespeare's Audience*. New York: Columbia University Press, 1941. An important account of the size and character of the typical audience when Shakespeare's plays were mounted at the Globe.

HILLEBRAND, H. N. *The Child Actors, A Chapter in Elizabethan Stage History*. New York: Russell and Russell, 1926. Full and reliable treatment of the subject.

HODGES, C. W. *The Globe Restored*. London: E. Benn, 1953. A modification of the influential theories of John C. Adams on the Globe Theatre.

HOTSON, LESLIE. *Shakespeare's Wooden O*. New York: The Macmillan Co., 1960.

JOSEPH, BERTRAM L. *Elizabethan Acting*. New York: Oxford University Press, 1951. An outstanding book on the subject. The author's thesis is that the performance of the Elizabethan actor was the same as that of the orator in the uses of voice, face, body, hands, and feet.

SPRAGUE, ARTHUR C. *Shakespeare and the Actor's Stage Business in His Plays (1600–1905)*. Cambridge, Mass.: Harvard University

Press, 1944. Expertly selected examples of the "business" of famous actors in crucial scenes of the plays. *Hamlet, Macbeth, Julius Caesar,* and *Romeo and Juliet* are treated.

STOPES, CHARLOTTE C. *Burbage and Shakespeare's Stage*. London: A. Moring, 1913. A thorough account of the poet's relation to James, Richard, and Cuthbert Burbage and the theatres in which Shakespeare's plays were acted.

V. GENERAL CRITICISM

BRADBY, ANNE (ed.). *Shakespeare Criticism 1919–1935*. New York: Oxford University Press, 1936.

BRADLEY, A. C. *Shakespearean Tragedy*. London: The Macmillan Co., 1904; New York: St. Martin's Press, 1955. The author gives memorable expression to the essential features of nineteenth-century criticism, i.e., the emphasis on the characters. An indispensable volume for understanding this one aspect of Shakespeare's work. It deals with *Hamlet, Othello, King Lear,* and *Macbeth.*

CAMPBELL, LILY B. *Shakespeare's Tragic Heroes*. New York: Cambridge University Press, 1930. This excellent study interprets the tragedies as expressions of Elizabethan psychology. Each one dramatizes a sickness of the soul: *Hamlet,* grief; *Othello,* jealousy; *King Lear,* wrath in old age.

CHARLTON, H. B. *Shakespearian Comedy*. New York: The Macmillan Co., 1938.

———. *Shakespearian Tragedy*. New York: Cambridge University Press, 1949.

CRAIG, HARDIN. *The Enchanted Glass; The Elizabethan Mind in Literature*. New York: Oxford University Press, 1950.

GRANVILLE-BARKER, H. *Prefaces to Shakespeare*. 2 vols. Princeton:

Princeton University Press, 1964. The author explains his ideas of the proper staging and acting of *Hamlet, King Lear, The Merchant of Venice, Antony and Cleopatra,* and *Cymbeline.*

MOULTON, RICHARD G. *Shakespeare as a Dramatic Artist.* 3d ed. New York: Oxford University Press, 1929. One of the best accounts of Shakespeare's methods in constructing his plays.

SMITH, D. N. (ed.). *Shakespeare Criticism: A Selection.* New York: Oxford University Press, 1916.

SPURGEON, CAROLINE F. E. *Shakespeare's Imagery and What It Tells Us.* New York: Cambridge University Press, 1935.

STAUFFER, DONALD. *Shakespeare's World of Images.* New York: W. W. Norton & Co., 1949. This book is a study of Shakespeare's formulation of ideas and moral attitudes in a single character, or in the tension established among two or more characters.

THORNDIKE, ASHLEY H. *English Comedy.* New York: The Macmillan Co., 1929. A substantial part of this book is devoted to Shakespeare's comedies and their relation to other plays.

WHITMORE, E. C.. *The Supernatural in Tragedy.* Cambridge, Mass.: Harvard University Press, 1915. The author treats the passage of the Senecan ghost into Elizabethan tragedy where it underwent a remarkable development, of which the ghost in *Hamlet* is the most famous example.

VI. A MIDSUMMER NIGHT'S DREAM

BARBER, C. I. *Shakespeare's Festival Comedy.* Princeton: Princeton University Press, 1959. The author shows that the "May Game" gave Shakespeare the pattern for all of the play's action. He converts Oberon, chief of the fairies, into the May King and thus presents the idea of a supernatural power at work in gadding maids and young men.

BRIGGS, KATHERINE. *The Anatomy of Puck*. New York: Oxford University Press, 1959. An examination of the extent to which Shakespeare's contemporaries believed in fairies.

EVANS, BERTRAND. *Shakespeare's Comedies*. New York: Oxford University Press, 1960.

HALLIWELL, J. O. *Memoranda on The Midsummer Night's Dream*. 1879. A collection of early documents of English fairy mythology, so far as they illustrate Shakespeare's conception of fairies; for example, extracts from Lord Berners' translation of "Huon de Bordeaux," and the Percy Society 1628 issue of *The Mad Pranks of Robin Goodfellow*, etc.

HUNTER, G. K. *William Shakespeare: The Late Comedies*. Deals with *A Midsummer Night's Dream, Much Ado About Nothing, As You Like It, Twelfth Night*. London: Longmans, Green, 1962.

LATHAM, MINOR W. *The Elizabethan Fairies*. New York: Columbia University Press, 1930. Shakespeare changes the homely, substantial, and formidable creatures of folk tradition into innocuous fairies, fit attendants of Oberon and Titania.

RICKERT, EDITH. "Political Propaganda and Satire in *A Midsummer-Night's Dream*." Modern Philology, XXI, pp. 53–54.

RITSON, JOSEPH. *Fairy Tales*, first collected, to which are prefixed two dissertions, 1) Pygmies; 2) Fairies. 1831. This collection was the result of the first critical investigation and discussion of fairies in England.

WILSON, JOHN DOVER. *Shakespeare's Happy Comedies*. London: Faber and Faber, 1962. The author's thesis is that we witness in the play an effect of the. midsummer madness that came to Elizabethan folk on Midsummer Night or St. John's Eve—the one season of the year when Elizabethan superstition was at its strongest. Everyone in the play was in some way affected by this midsummer madness.